Why Wills Won't Work

(IF YOU WANT TO PROTECT YOUR ASSETS)

AVERY   A MEMBER OF PENGUIN GROUP (USA) INC.   NEW YORK

Why Wills Won't Work

(IF YOU WANT TO PROTECT YOUR ASSETS)

Safeguard Your Estate for the
Ones You Really Love

Armond D. Budish

Published by the Penguin Group
Penguin Group (USA) Inc., 375 Hudson Street, New York, New York 10014, USA •
Penguin Group (Canada), 90 Eglinton Avenue East, Suite 700, Toronto, Ontario M4P 2Y3, Canada
(a division of Pearson Penguin Canada Inc.) • Penguin Books Ltd, 80 Strand, London WC2R 0RL,
England • Penguin Ireland, 25 St Stephen's Green, Dublin 2, Ireland (a division of Penguin Books Ltd) •
Penguin Group (Australia), 250 Camberwell Road, Camberwell, Victoria 3124,
Australia (a division of Pearson Australia Group Pty Ltd) • Penguin Books India Pvt Ltd,
11 Community Centre, Panchsheel Park, New Delhi–110 017, India • Penguin Group (NZ),
67 Apollo Drive, Mairangi Bay, Auckland 1311, New Zealand (a division of
Pearson New Zealand Ltd) • Penguin Books (South Africa) (Pty) Ltd,
24 Sturdee Avenue, Rosebank, Johannesburg 2196, South Africa

Penguin Books Ltd, Registered Offices: 80 Strand, London WC2R 0RL, England

Most Avery books are available at special quantity discounts for bulk purchase for sales promotions, premiums, fund-raising, and educational needs. Special books or book excerpts also can be created to fit specific needs. For details, write Penguin Group (USA) Inc. Special Markets, 375 Hudson Street, New York, NY 10014.

Library of Congress Cataloging-in-Publication Data

Budish, Armond D.
Why wills won't work (if you want to protect your assets):
safeguard your estate for the ones you really love / Armond D. Budish.
p.   cm.
Includes index.
ISBN 978-1-58333-273-3
1. Estate planning—United States—Popular works.
I. Title.   II. Title: Freedom, asset protection, and the individual.
KF750.Z9B84   2007   2006037025
346.7305'2—dc22

Printed in the United States of America
1   3   5   7   9   10   8   6   4   2

BOOK DESIGN BY NICOLE LAROCHE

This publication is designed to provide accurate and authoritative information in regard to the subject matter covered. It is sold with the understanding that the publisher is not engaged in rendering legal, accounting, or other professional services. If you require legal advice or other expert assistance, you should seek the services of a competent professional.

While the author has made every effort to provide accurate telephone numbers and Internet addresses at the time of publication, neither the publisher nor the author assumes any responsibility for errors, or for changes that occur after publication. Further, the publisher does not have any control over and does not assume any responsibility for author or third-party websites or their content.

Contents

Author's Note

A number of accomplished attorneys made significant contributions to the success of this book and the SAFE approach to estate preservation. These include:

Michael Gilfix

Michael Gilfix is a cofounder and Fellow of the National Academy of Elder Law Attorneys (NAELA). In 1973, he created the first legal aid program for seniors, and in 1983 he established the law firm that is today known as Gilfix & LaPoll Associates LLP. Gilfix has been a principal speaker for numerous trust and tax symposia at the national level, including the Center for Judicial Education, the American Institute of Certified Public Accountants, and the New York University Tax Institute. Gilfix is coauthor of *Tax, Estate & Financial Planning for the Elderly: Forms and Practice* (Matthew Bender), and he regularly contributes to a wide variety of legal journals such as *Trusts & Estates magazine*. Gilfix's office is located in Palo Alto, California.

A. Frank Johns

A. Frank Johns is past president and fellow in NAELA and currently sits as chair of NAELA's Council of Advanced Practitioners. He is board certified by the National Elder Law Foundation and a registered guardian. He was a charter board member of the National Guardianship Association and is a fellow in the American College of Trust and Estate Counsel. Johns was the charter chair of the North Carolina Bar Association Elder Law Section, and he coauthored the second edition of *Counseling Older Clients* (ALI/ABA 2005). Johns serves as chair of the advisory board of the Masters of Gerontology/MBA Dual Degree Program at the University of North Carolina at Greensboro, where he is a visiting associate professor. Johns is a charter partner in Booth Harrington & Johns LLP, with offices in Charlotte and Greensboro, North Carolina. He is a board member of Senior Resources of Guilford, president of the board of the Western Carolina Chapter of the Alzheimer's Association, and board member of the Society of Financial Service Professionals, Greensboro Chapter.

Bernard A. Krooks

Bernard Krooks is a past president and fellow of the National Academy of Elder Law Attorneys and president of the academy's New York chapter. He is past chair of the Elder Law Section of the New York State Bar Association and a fellow of the American College of Trust and Estate Counsel. He is a board member of the Westchester Arc and a member of the Blythedale Children's Hospital Planned Giving Professional Advisory Board, and he has served on the board of directors of the Alzheimer's Association Westchester/Putnam chapter. Krooks is an adjunct assistant professor at New York University Center for Finance, Law, and Taxation. A sought-after expert on elder-law matters, Krooks has been quoted in *The Wall Street Journal, The New York Times, Money, SmartMoney, Lawyers Weekly USA, Reader's Digest*, the *New York Law Journal, Newsweek*, the *Journal of Financial Planning*, and *Newsday*, among other publications. He has testified before the U.S. House of Representatives and the New York City Council on long-term care issues. He has appeared as an elder law expert on National Public Radio, PBS, NBC, and CBS. He is a founding partner of the law firm of Littman Krooks LLP, with offices in New York City and White Plains, New York.

Harry S. Margolis

Harry Margolis is the founder and president of ElderLawAnswers, the premier Web site resource with information about various legal issues facing seniors and their families. He is also the editor of *The ElderLaw Report,* an essential newsletter for attorneys, and author of the *ElderLaw Forms Manual.* Margolis is a fellow of the National Academy of Elder Law Attorneys and founding president of the academy's Massachusetts chapter. Like Armond Budish, he is a graduate of Swarthmore College and New York University Law School. He is the founder of his law firm, Margolis & Associates, located in Boston.

Vincent J. Russo

Vincent Russo is a founding member, fellow, and past president of NAELA and a founding member and past chair of the Elder Law Section of the New York State Bar Association. He is a past board member and president of the Guardianship Committee of the United Cerebral Palsy Association of Nassau and a founding member and officer of the Theresa Alessandra Russo Foundation for children with special needs. Russo is a cofounder of the Academy of Special Needs Planners as well as a noted author on the subjects of elder law and estate planning. His articles have been published in the *New York State Bar Journal, Trusts & Estates* magazine, and the *NAELA Journal.* He was featured on the cover of *Financial Planning,* has been a guest on *Today* on NBC, and has appeared on multiple radio and television programs, including CNN, CNBC, the FOX News Network, C-SPAN II, and News 12 Long Island, addressing the issues and concerns of the elderly and persons with disabilities. Mr. Russo is the managing shareholder of his law firm, Vincent J. Russo & Associates, P.C., with offices in Westbury, Islandia, Lido Beach, and Woodbury, New York.

Mike Solomon, Laurie Steiner, and Jennifer Peck

Mike Solomon, Laurie Steiner, and Jennifer Peck are Armond Budish's law partners and worked closely with Armond in developing SAFE Trusts and the SAFE approach to planning. Without their support, expertise, and guidance, this book could not have been written.

Mike Solomon received his law degree and master's in tax law from Georgetown University Law Center. He worked for the national office of the IRS before entering private practice. Solomon is a frequent speaker locally and nationally on tax and business topics, and he cochaired the American Bar Association National Institutes on Pension Issues.

Laurie Steiner received her law degree from Cleveland Marshall College of Law, magna cum laude. She is a frequent speaker on elder law, asset protection, and Medicaid planning topics, and she is a contributing author to *Fifty Something Magazine*. Steiner is a frequent guest and substitute host for the television program *Golden Opportunities*.

Jennifer Peck is a certified specialist in estate planning, trust, and probate law by the Ohio State Bar Association. She received her law degree from Cleveland Marshall College of Law, cum laude. Peck has taught "Legal Issues and the Elderly" at Cuyahoga Community College and is a frequent lecturer for professional and community programs. She was working on her master's in tax law when she decided to pursue two other more interesting matters—her daughters.

INTRODUCTION

Where Will All Your Money Go After You're Gone?

While you are alive and well, you have the power to control
your money—you hold the purse strings, and you decide
how to invest and spend those dollars. That's simple enough.

Then what happens? Just as it does with every other human in the history of the world, no matter how rich or famous, death will eventually come knocking at your door. And you must answer, leaving behind all your family, friends, and worldly goods. Although none of us yet has the power to change this inevitable conclusion, we *do* have the ability to control *where* our money goes after we're gone. And that's why this book will work for you. SAFE Trusts will empower you to do the best possible planning for the future.

If you are like most people I work with, your number-one concern is to protect your family and to assure that the inheritance you've worked so hard to build will be completely secure for your spouse, your children, your grandchildren, and other intended heirs.

You may think that you've taken care of your loved ones by making a will. Many years ago, preparing a will probably was enough, and this book would not have been necessary. But let me be perfectly clear: those days are over. If you use a will to pass assets to your heirs, you have condemned your family to months, sometimes years, of paperwork, fees, and costs, by forcing your estate into probate court. That's one key reason why *a will won't work* to protect assets for your family.

There are three common ways to leave your life savings to your family while *avoiding* the hassles and expense of probate. They are: (1) joint ownership, (2) beneficiary designations, and (3) a Revocable Living Trust. Joint ownership and beneficiary designations are easy to do. Just go to the bank or broker and name your spouse, children, or others as co-owners or beneficiaries on your accounts. At your death, these accounts will pass to your heirs simply and quickly, without probate. But these planning techniques often cause unexpected, costly problems, which can create headaches for you, and even lead to the breakup of good family relationships. We'll explain in detail in Chapter 1 why joint ownership and beneficiary designations won't work to protect your family.

Millions of Americans have sought to bypass probate *and* avoid the problems of joint or beneficiary ownership by creating a Revocable Living Trust. A Revocable Living Trust is the most common, standard type of trust. (There are actually many different types of trusts, which provide many different benefits, and we'll talk about them in the coming chapters.) The Revocable Living Trust is a legal document that looks a lot like a will, stating where your assets are to go when you die. When you put your house, accounts, and other investments into a Revocable Living Trust during your life (called funding the trust, discussed in Chapter 7), the trust enables your family to avoid probate when you pass on.

The popularity of Revocable Living Trusts soared after the 1965 publication by Norman Dacey of his bestselling book *How to Avoid Probate!* and continues even now. Yes, Revocable Living Trusts do work well to avoid probate. But, again, avoiding probate does not mean your assets are adequately protected for your heirs. Joint ownership, beneficiary designations, and Revocable Living Trusts are no longer enough. These twentieth-century estate-planning tools all fail to provide the protections needed to cope with twenty-first-century estate-busting problems.

Let's take just one key concern: providing an inheritance for your children. Not a single one of these traditional tools can protect your legacy from being grabbed by a child's spouse if your child gets a divorce or when he/she dies: leaving your assets to heirs under a will won't work; naming joint owners won't work; designating beneficiaries won't work; even creating a Revocable Living Trust won't work. The bottom line is always the same: once your heirs get the inheritance, your money and property belong to them. At first that may be okay. But if your child later gets a divorce, and the former spouse winds up with half of the inheritance meant for your child, is that still okay? If your child dies after receiving the inheritance, and *all* your money goes to the child's spouse (who might remarry and share that inheritance with a new spouse), is that still okay?

Consider the following real-life estate nightmares resulting from inadequate planning:

Susan's Story

At her death, Susan left her home and savings to her daughter, Diana. Diana was deeply appreciative, because money was tight. Her husband, Rob, was just starting work as an attorney, and she had quit her job after the birth of their first child.

Just as Rob's career was starting to take off, he surprised Diana by moving out and filing for a divorce. Diana's surprise later turned to shock when the judge decreed that all the couple's assets, including the inheritance from her mother, were to be split down the middle. The last thing Susan would have wanted was for half of her hard-earned life savings to wind up with Diana's ex-husband. Susan would probably roll over in her grave if she knew that all her good intentions had been undermined by poor planning.

Having your hard-earned life savings eventually pass to your children's spouses isn't the only defect in traditional twentieth-century estate planning. Today we live in a litigious society; people sue one another for all sorts of reasons. If you wish to protect your estate for your loved ones, your planning must also include protections against creditors and lawsuits. Take a look at the story of Elaine.

Elaine's Story

Elaine knew her son's landscaping company was not doing well. Dave was a wonderful person but lacked business savvy. She periodically helped him out of his money problems. She needed most of her savings, though, to generate the interest income that she drew on to live. Elaine hoped that the inheritance she'd leave Dave would secure his future.

Unfortunately, that's not how things worked out. At her death, Dave inherited about $200,000. Within months, his creditors who were owed money filed lawsuits and eventually gobbled up most of Elaine's legacy. The inheritance that Elaine had intended to serve as a financial safety net for her son had disappeared.

Standard wills, joint and beneficiary accounts, and Revocable Living Trusts also will not provide other needed safeguards, including:

- Protecting your life savings when you or your spouse gets sick and needs nursing home care.
- Preventing your spouse from squandering the inheritance you intended for your kids.
- Ensuring that your younger (or immature) child won't blow the funds intended for his/her education, a home, or a business.
- Providing management and safeguarding public benefits for a child with special needs.
- Sheltering your hard-earned money from the tax collector, not just during your life, but at your death as well, and again when your kids pass on.

Fortunately, the estate nightmares that befell Susan's and Elaine's families, as well as many more we haven't discussed yet, don't have to ruin the dreams you have for *your* heirs. There is a solution: the next generation estate planning strategy for a new generation of Americans. *It's* called "SAFE" planning, designed to *Safeguard* *Assets* for your *Family* *Exclusively*.

For twenty years I have been assisting families in protecting their homes and life savings, and in fulfilling their dreams, through estate planning. In the mid-1980s I became one of the first attorneys in the country to focus on the field of elder law. My books *Avoiding the Medicaid Trap: How to Beat the Catastrophic Costs of Nursing Home Care* and *Golden Opportunities: Hundreds of Money-Making, Money-Saving Gems for Anyone over Fifty* quickly became national bibles on family asset maximization and protection. I have served as a contributing editor of *Family Circle* magazine, and I created and host a weekly television program for fifty-plusers called *Golden Opportunities*.

While helping thousands of people plan for their futures, I have come to see that the common, traditional estate-planning approaches and tools typically utilized in the twentieth century no longer provide the necessary solutions to our twenty-first-century problems. I saw hardworking people who wanted to do the best for their families, yet were woefully misinformed or, even worse, misled about how to protect those they loved. Often, people would come into my law office, asking for a will or a Revocable Living Trust, without having considered their goals, without recognizing the dangers awaiting their families, and without even understanding what those documents can and cannot do. In response to people's frustration and confusion with the process of traditional estate planning, I developed the SAFE approach to estate planning.

Wills, joint and beneficiary ownership, and Revocable Living Trusts are *tools,* not solutions to problems. When you're building a home, you don't go to a builder and pick out a particular hammer; instead, you'd first go to an architect, explain your hopes and dreams (and of course, your budget), and ask for help creating a plan. When you're not feeling well, you don't go to the doctor and tell him you want a particular medication or surgery; no, you would tell him or her about your problem, you'd be given a checkup, and then you would be presented with a treatment plan.

What sets SAFE planning apart is that it is a comprehensive, holistic approach to your estate concerns. You are a partner in the process: its creation requires your active participation.

Good estate planning does not simply involve filling in the blanks on a legal form. It is not a one-size-fits-all project. The "old style" estate planning is document-driven; twenty-first-century estate planning must be problem-driven and solution-driven, and it requires a thoughtful examination and analysis of your family's needs, risks, and goals.

This book will walk you through the ABC's of a SAFE plan:

- Assessment of your family's relationships, assets, needs, and goals.
- Breakdown of the most beneficial options available to build your plan.
- Comprehensive solution to protect your family.

In Chapter 2, you will find the fifty-question SAFE Assessment Tool, to help you identify your needs and goals. The questions are not difficult, but they require your considered thought and honest answers. They include:

What is your relationship with your children? Do the children get along with one another? Do they work outside the home? Do any of them have special issues, such as problems with drugs, alcohol, or gambling? Is any child disabled? How are they at managing money? Are the kids married? Do you like the spouses? Are there grandchildren?

Once you've identified your needs and goals, with the help of the SAFE Assessment Tool, we'll present you with a breakdown of the best options available to address and avoid future problems. You'll be amazed to learn that with SAFE planning and in particular with SAFE Trusts, you *can* keep your inheritance from your children's spouses, their creditors, and the tax man; you *can* insulate your estate from second marriages, lawsuits, and nursing home costs; you *can* protect young, immature, and disabled beneficiaries; and you can provide for charities while protecting your family, with Uncle Sam's help. And finally, this book will empower you to develop the comprehensive solutions that are required to protect our families in the twenty-first century.

SAFE planning is more involved, and can be more expensive, than traditional estate planning. You'll need a lawyer to assist and guide you; SAFE planning is not a do-it-yourself area. The legal fees for a traditional Revocable Living Trust may run $1,500 to $3,000; adding a SAFE Trust may increase your cost by $1,500 or more. SAFE planning is not for everyone. While it is more expensive, it is also far more beneficial than old-style planning. There is *no* other way to protect the inheritance you wish to leave for your children and grandchildren from their spouses, creditors, lawsuits, and taxes. In this book I will walk you through every step of the process to assure that the secure future you envision for your family is not lost or stolen from you. All the answers you'll need can be found between these covers.

PART I

Twenty-First-Century Planning

CHAPTER 1

Why Wills
Won't Work

Are you "willing" to bet your home and entire life's savings on the fact that you're adequately protected with a will? Let's hope not, because that's a bet you'd probably lose. While it's long been said that "everyone should have a will," a will cannot provide your family with all of the twenty-first-century protections you want and need. So let's put to rest the five most costly estate-draining myths about what wills do.

Myth 1: A will will avoid probate

Unfortunately, this is not true.

Here's what *will* happen if you leave your estate to your heirs with a will: everything you own will pass through probate. Despite what many people think, wills do *not* avoid probate.

What exactly is probate, and why does it have such a bad reputation? In a nutshell, probate is the system designed to assure that a person's money and property are legally transferred to the right heirs at his or her death—at least that's the nice way to describe it. It begins with the filing of the will with the local probate court. Immediate family members and beneficiaries named in the will must be notified. Anyone wishing to challenge the will may do so.

Once the will is filed, it must be verified as legitimate. In your will, you can nominate an executor (sometimes called an administrator or personal representative), who will be appointed by the probate court to handle the estate (unless there is some strong reason not to appoint your nominee). From that point on, everything done in the estate usually must be overseen and approved by the probate judge.

In most states, here's what happens: the executor typically must make a list of everything owned by the deceased at death—every bank account, stock, bond, money market, mutual fund, and piece of real estate. The list is filed with the court, which makes it public record—anyone in the world can take a look at the will and assets. Every transaction, every purchase, every sale of an asset must be reported to the court. All income received after the death, including interest, dividends, and rents, must be listed and every expenditure, including home owner's insurance, utilities, and taxes, must be approved by the court. All this takes time. There's a mountain of paperwork to prepare and submit. Typically the executor must hire a lawyer to help, and as you know, lawyers don't work for free.

A 1990 study of probate by the AARP concluded that probate is "costly, slow, outmoded . . . [a] sad state of affairs." The report first focused on costs, finding that "for the estates of the middle class . . . fees can deplete the assets by as much as 10 percent even in uncomplicated cases." (*A Report on Probate: Consumer Perspectives and Concerns,* Washington, D.C.: AARP, 1990).

Costs are only part of the problem. The same AARP study found that probate of estates under $100,000 took, on average, well over a year. Why so long? Most of the delay lies in the paperwork that must be completed in order to comply with the state laws that have multiple deadlines and requirements.

While the AARP report was published seventeen years ago, sadly not much has changed. Although the system was designed to protect your estate at death, it more often than not can be an "estate buster." That's why most people hate probate. While there are estate-planning techniques designed to *avoid* probate, wills are not one of those techniques.

Myth 2: A will will protect my young children

If you leave your estate to children, they'll get it upon your death. If they are young, you may name a guardian and/or custodian in a will to manage for them until they reach the legal age of maturity, typically eighteen or twenty-one. But under a will, that's it—they get the inheritance no later than age twenty-one. Ready or not, the money is theirs to spend, on cars, trips, parties, all the things you might have said no to if you had been alive. For many children, even the "ripe old age" of twenty-one is too young to receive an inheritance outright.

For example, let's take a look at Mark's case. Mark's parents died when he was quite young, leaving him with an inheritance of about $150,000. Mark's aunt and uncle raised him and managed the inheritance for him. On Mark's twenty-first birthday, the assets became his, and Mark decided to reward himself for what had been a pretty tough life. He spent the next year having a great time traveling through Europe, and enjoying the "sights" at every local pub. Against the sound advice of his aunt and uncle, Mark went through his inheritance money faster than a smooth ale.

By age twenty-five, Mark had became somewhat wiser. He decided that finishing college now would be a good idea. Regrettably, this sobering realization came too late; he had foolishly squandered his inheritance.

Myth 3: A will will protect the inheritance from my child's spouse or creditors

Lots of folks think they have protected their children and grandchildren by putting the language *per stirpes* in their will. They're wrong. *Per stirpes* is Latin, meaning "by roots." In practice, it means that if your child dies *before* you, then at your death the child's share will pass to your deceased child's children and *not* to your deceased child's spouse. So to a very limited extent, it does keep the inheritance in your bloodline.

But thankfully, the chance of your children dying *before* you is small. It's much more likely that your children will outlive you. When that's the case, *per stirpes* is useless. At your death, any living children will get their share. Outright. If they later get a divorce, or die, some or all of the inheritance may go to the child's spouse. And if they're sued, all of the inheritance is jeopardized.

Myth 4: A will will protect my estate from nursing homes

A will is useless until you die. If you go to a nursing home, you're alive, and the will provides no protection. Most or all of your estate may be used for your bills. You *can* protect at least part of your life savings from nursing homes and for your family, but a will is not the solution.

Myth 5: A will will protect me in case I become incapacitated

If you become incompetent and can't handle your own finances, you must give someone else the authority during your lifetime to handle your finances for you—to withdraw money from your accounts, take distributions from your IRAs, sell stocks, refinance your home, pay your bills. A will does not take effect until you die, so it *cannot* protect you if you become incompetent.

I hope that we've dispelled those dangerous myths about the protections that a will provides for you and your family. Now, don't get me wrong. Even in twenty-first-century SAFE planning, you'll still need a simple will. This will, often called a Pourover Will, coordinates closely with your SAFE planning. It serves as a safety net, placing assets in your SAFE Trust at death if you failed to fund your trust during life. And when a will is combined with SAFE planning, you should be able to avoid the downsides we've just discussed. (See Chapter 8 for more about the use of a will.)

It's not enough just to reveal the defects in wills. The other most common estate-planning tools—joint ownership, beneficiary designations, and Revocable Living Trusts—also will not work to adequately protect the inheritance intended for *your* family. Let's examine each one.

JOINT OWNERSHIP

The most common way to avoid probate is joint ownership. You may be holding lots of your assets jointly right now, such as your home jointly with your spouse, or bank accounts jointly with the kids. Just take a look at your house deed, stock certificate, or account statement to see whose name is on it. You can choose to hold almost any assets with someone else jointly with "rights of survivorship." While both owners are alive, both own and control the property. When one dies, the survivor owns the asset automatically, without the need to go through probate. It's fast, it's easy, it's inexpensive— and I generally don't recommend it.

Perhaps between husband and wife, joint ownership will work out okay—depending on their relationship. But joint ownership with anyone else—children, nephews, nieces, siblings—is *very* dangerous.

Let me give you three true stories that illustrate just a few of the dangers of joint ownership.

Mary's Story

Mary put her daughter Julie on her house deed, so that it would pass to her without probate at her death. Several years later, Mary decided she wanted to sell the house and move into an apartment. She found a buyer who offered a good price, and she was ready to finalize the sale. The only problem was: Julie's husband wouldn't agree. Even though he wasn't named on the deed, as a spouse he became an owner, under Mary's state's law, as soon as Mary named Julie on the deed. Julie's husband was not a good person, and just to be spiteful he blocked the sale, causing Mary a lot of heartache and a significant financial loss.

Harry's Story

Harry put his son Frank on his brokerage account. This was done for two reasons: Harry wanted some help handling his finances and he wanted to avoid probate when he died. It all sounded good on paper.

Unfortunately, when Harry went to take $20,000 to buy a new car, he discovered the account had been closed. Frank had taken the money. Turns out Frank had a gambling problem. I guess Frank just "forgot" to ask his dad's permission before emptying his account!

Laurel's Story

Then there was the case of Laurel and her daughter, Sara. Laurel and her daughter had a wonderful relationship; Sara was an ideal child. No chance she'd steal her mother's money. But it turns out the problem wasn't with Sara.

To Laurel's surprise, Sara was sued by her husband for divorce. Sara's soon-to-be ex-hubby hired a good lawyer, who did what most lawyers do. He asked for and obtained from the domestic relations judge an order freezing every asset that had Sara's name on it. The legal rationale for this is to protect marital assets, so an angry spouse can't run to the bank, pull out all the money, and either hide or spend the funds. The freeze applied to all assets with Sara's name, including Laurel's account.

Laurel had the right to hire a lawyer, go to the domestic relations judge, set a hearing, and present evidence that the joint account was really Laurel's money. She did that, and the judge unfroze that account so that Laurel could obtain her money. But the process took *almost a year* (courts often don't move very fast). And during that time Laurel couldn't touch her own funds. It was a good thing the freeze was eventually lifted, because Laurel needed every penny to pay the lawyer who helped her win the case.

I could fill this book with more horror stories, but I think you get the point. Joint ownership is dangerous. It can "dis-joint" you from your assets in ways you never expected.

BENEFICIARY DESIGNATIONS

The second way to avoid probate is to name beneficiaries. You've probably done this on your life insurance, IRAs, and 401(k)s. You fill out a form, naming who should get the assets at your death. When you die, the money or property passes to the named beneficiaries with *no* probate.

You can name beneficiaries on almost anything: checking, savings and CDs (often called Payable on Death accounts), stocks, mutual funds, and brokerage accounts (often called Transfer on Death accounts), and in many states, even on your real estate (often called a Transfer on Death deed). Beneficiary designations, like joint ownership, are easy and inexpensive. And they're a lot safer than naming a joint owner. With beneficiary designations, no one has any rights to your property until you die.

You can avoid the problem that Mary had with Julie's husband when he refused to sign off on the house sale. You can avoid Harry's problem of having a child clear out the accounts. And unlike Laurel, you can avoid having your assets frozen during a divorce.

But beneficiary designations are not perfect. They can still cause headaches and heartaches. Here's one true case that illustrates one of the problems that can arise.

Roberta's Story

Roberta named her three children as beneficiaries on her house deed. They had *no* rights while Roberta lived. At her death, the home transferred directly and immediately to her three children. No fuss, no muss, and no probate.

At that point, the three kids owned the home. But that wasn't all. Their three spouses also owned the home (under their state's law). No decision could be made regarding the home without the *unanimous* agreement of all six owners—no majority votes. With six people's opinions, what are the odds of unanimity without animosity?

Should they do some fixing up and make repairs before the house is put on the market? Six people had to agree.

What items should be fixed, and how much should be paid? Six people had to agree.

Should they try selling by owner, or hire a real estate agent? Six people had to agree.

How much should they ask? Six people had to agree.

When an offer came in, should they accept, reject, or make a counteroffer? Six people had to agree.

How much should they counter? Six people had to agree.

I'm sure you're getting the idea. Naming beneficiaries on your house deed can be the best way to leave the home and avoid probate—*if* you want the roof to cave in on family accord after you're gone. Fortunately, there's a better way.

STARTER TRUST

The third way to avoid probate is a Starter Trust. We've given it the name Starter Trust because it's the starting point for many more complex planning tools. Lots of people have heard of Revocable Living Trusts, which are the most common type of Starter Trusts, but few really understand what they are and how they work. Here we'll explain how Revocable Living Trusts work; in Chapters 4 and 5 we'll tell you about other useful Starter Trusts.

A Revocable Living Trust is a very useful legal document that looks and acts somewhat like a will. Like a will, it states that, upon your death, your assets will pass to your spouse, your children, or other designated heirs. But unlike a will, because your assets are held in the trust, you avoid probate.

Picture a Revocable Living Trust like a big box or a storage trunk. You can put assets into the trunk while you are alive. Stocks, bonds, mutual funds, CDs, real estate, cars—almost anything you own can go into the box. This is called "funding the trust" and is discussed in more detail in Chapter 7.

In most cases, *you* can be in control of the box or trunk, by naming yourself as the trustee of your Revocable Living Trust, and that's the way most people set it up. The trustee is the manager, the boss. While you're alive, all of the assets in the Revocable Living Trust remain yours. As trustee, you can handle the investments, buy CDs, sell stocks, and do whatever else is necessary to manage the investments. You can spend your money, live in the home, and drive the car. You can give things away that are in the storage trunk; you can put more things into storage whenever you wish. You have control during your lifetime. You can continue to conduct your financial affairs under a Revocable Living Trust just as you always have. And you can change or cancel the trust at any time—that's why it's called revocable.

Lots of folks used to be scared away from trusts, because they thought a bank trustee had to be in charge. That's the way it used to be. But today, most people choose to be their own trustee. Keep in mind that even if you choose to serve as your own trustee, you will need a backup to take over should you become incapacitated or when you die. You can name your spouse, your kids, and/or other family members as alternate trustees of a Revocable Living Trust.

Of course, you can choose an institutional trustee, like a bank or brokerage firm. In some cases, this is appropriate. For example, if you don't want the hassles of management, you may opt for an institutional trustee while you're still alive. You could also decide to serve as your own trustee, while naming a bank as alternate to manage for your spouse when you're gone. But most folks opt to keep the job of trustee "all in the family." We'll talk more about selecting trustees in Chapter 7.

Revocable Living Trusts can be used by and for you, and they last up until you die. At your death, the storage trunk typically empties out. Its contents pass to the folks that you've designated as heirs: usually a spouse, children, charities, or others.

The primary purpose of a Revocable Living Trust is to avoid probate at death. When the box empties at your death, and the items are distributed to your heirs, there's no probate.

A Revocable Living Trust works: it avoids the costs, hassles, and delays of probate at death. It's safer than joint ownership, because no one else owns your assets while you're alive. You can make sure that only you can control, take, and spend your money until death. And a Revocable Living Trust avoids the problems of beneficiary designations as well. For example, you can avoid the type of problems encountered by Roberta's family by naming one child to serve as trustee when you're gone, with the power to make decisions concerning the sale of the home. Only after the sale do your kids get the proceeds.

At your death, your spouse or kids get whatever you have gifted to them from the Revocable Living Trust. It's quick, and it's pretty easy. A standard Revocable Living Trust document does not have to be complicated. In fact, Dacey's book *How to Avoid Probate!* included fill-in-the-blank Revocable Living Trust forms.

To fill out a simple Revocable Living Trust, relatively few questions must be answered. The primary ones are: who should take over and manage your assets if you become incapacitated; where do your assets go when you die; and where do your assets go if your first choice(s) for beneficiary died before you. Almost any lawyer can do this (and most do); even non-lawyer "trust mills" have (improperly) gotten into the business of preparing Revocable Living Trusts.

But don't be confused—filling in the blanks on a Revocable Living Trust form is not comprehensive, thorough estate planning. To say that creating a Revocable Living Trust is a complete estate plan is like saying that putting all your money in your checking account is a comprehensive financial investment plan. By itself, a Revocable Living Trust fails to protect your children and grandchildren from many risks and dangers, both known and unknown; and it won't work to protect your estate from attacks by in-laws, creditors, and tax collectors.

Typically, a Revocable Living Trust simply distributes assets to your children after you die. And that's where the problems start to arise. Once your children get the inheritance, it's theirs, no strings attached, no exceptions. You money is now in their names and becomes part of *their* lives, for better or worse. Revocable Living Trusts themselves provide *no* protections for your children or grandchildren in case they divorce, or die, or are sued. In many cases, your inheritance ends up with a child's spouse or creditors.

Lots of people over the years have used wills, joint ownership, beneficiary designations, and Revocable Living Trusts to pass their assets to their heirs at death. Lots of folks thought they had adequately planned

REVOCABLE LIVING TRUST
You serve as your own trustee and retain control

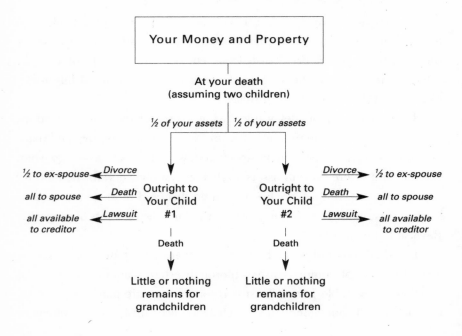

their estates and protected their families. And lots of folks made terrible, costly mistakes. In today's world, one out of two marriages ends in divorce, and soon-to-be ex-in-laws are not reluctant to grab as much as possible; our society is more litigious than ever; and taxes continue to eat away at our savings. These new realities call for a new, comprehensive, twenty-first-century response that will more completely protect your legacy for future generations of your family.

CHAPTER 2

Assessing Your Family's Needs

A good estate plan that *truly* protects you and your family requires a holistic review of your entire personal, financial, and legal situation. Pulling a document off the Internet and filling in the blanks is *not* a good plan. Buying a book and tearing out the form is *not* a good plan. Seeing a lawyer who prepares a will or trust for you without asking about your health, your spouse, your children and grandchildren, your in-laws, your income and expenses, and, most important, your hopes and dreams is *not* a good plan.

A good estate plan, a SAFE plan to safeguard your family, begins with a thorough assessment of your family's resources, needs, and goals. To help collect the necessary facts and figures, ascertain your concerns, and uncover potential problems lurking in the shadows, we have provided a specially designed SAFE Assessment Tool ("SAT").

To maximize its value, you must think about each question and answer fully—and honestly. This is not the time to pretend your family is more perfect than Ozzie and Harriet's or the Huxtables'. If your daughter is a spendthrift, say so. If your son's wife is not very nice to you, say so. If your spouse's children from his first marriage won't talk to you, say so. You don't have to describe the scenario in lurid detail complete with unprintable expletives, but do give an accurate picture.

In preparation for taking your SAT, gather your recent checking, savings, CD and brokerage statements, insurance policies, real estate titles, tax bills and appraisals, check registers, utility bills, loan balances, prescription drug list, and address book. These will help you answer many of the questions.

Don't worry about how your answers sound. There are no right or wrong responses. You cannot fail this SAT! After you've filled out the SAFE Assessment Tool, we'll explain why we asked the questions and the significance of your answers.

SAFE ASSESSMENT TOOL

1. **YOU**   **SPOUSE (IF MARRIED)**

NAME: _____   _____

ADDRESS: _____   _____

TELEPHONE: _____   _____

CELL PHONE: _____   _____

2. WHAT IS THE DATE OF BIRTH FOR:

YOU   ___ / ___ / ___   **SPOUSE**   ___ / ___ / ___

3. WHAT IS YOUR MARITAL STATUS?

___ MARRIED ___ NEVER MARRIED ___ WIDOWED ___ DIVORCED

4. IS THIS THE FIRST MARRIAGE FOR:

YOU   ___ YES   ___ NO

SPOUSE   ___ YES   ___ NO

5. HOW LONG HAVE YOU BEEN MARRIED TO YOUR CURRENT SPOUSE?

_____

6. IS THERE ANY PERTINENT INFORMATION ABOUT YOUR HEALTH? IN-
CLUDE ANY RECENT SURGERIES, AND LIST ANY HEALTH CONDITIONS
FOR WHICH YOU ARE TAKING MEDICATIONS. _____

_____

_____

_____

_____

7. IS THERE ANY PERTINENT INFORMATION ABOUT YOUR SPOUSE'S
HEALTH STATUS? _____

_____

_____

8. DO YOU OR YOUR SPOUSE HAVE ANY CONDITIONS THAT LIMIT
YOUR DAILY ACTIVITIES (E.G., ARTHRITIS OR LOSS OF BALANCE THAT
REQUIRES USE OF A CANE; FORGETFULNESS THAT REQUIRES ASSIS-
TANCE TAKING MEDICATIONS)? IF SO, LIST EACH LIMITATION, ALONG
WITH ANY ACCOMMODATION USED. _____

_____

_____

_____

_____

9. IF YOU HAVE CHILDREN AND/OR GRANDCHILDREN, LIST EACH OF
THEIR NAMES, AGES, ADDRESSES, TELEPHONE NUMBERS, AND MARI-
TAL STATUS. _____

_____

_____

_____

_____

10. ARE ANY OF YOUR CHILDREN NOT THE CHILDREN OF YOUR CURRENT SPOUSE? IF SO, PLEASE NAME THEM. _____

_____

_____

_____

11. IF YOUR SPOUSE HAS CHILDREN WHO ARE NOT YOURS, PLEASE LIST YOUR SPOUSE'S CHILDREN AND GRANDCHILDREN. _____

_____

_____

_____

_____

(FOR ALL FUTURE QUESTIONS REFERRING TO YOUR CHILDREN, INCLUDE YOUR AND YOUR SPOUSE'S CHILDREN.)

12. CREATE A ONE- OR TWO-SENTENCE PROFILE FOR EACH OF YOUR CHILDREN (I.E., EXPLAIN WHAT YOU THINK OF THEM, INCLUDING THEIR STRONGEST AND WEAKEST POINTS; DESCRIBE YOUR RELATIONSHIP WITH THEM). BE HONEST! _____

_____

_____

_____

_____

_____

13. CREATE A ONE- OR TWO-SENTENCE PROFILE FOR EACH SPOUSE OR SIGNIFICANT OTHER OF EACH OF YOUR CHILDREN (I.E., EXPLAIN WHAT YOU THINK OF THEM, INCLUDING THEIR STRONGEST AND WEAKEST POINTS; DESCRIBE YOUR RELATIONSHIPS WITH THEM). BE HONEST!

_____

_____

_____

_____

14. DO ANY OF YOUR CHILDREN OR THEIR SPOUSES HAVE PROBLEMS WITH:

_____ ALCOHOL   (WHO? _____)

_____ DRUGS   (WHO? _____)

_____ GAMBLING   (WHO? _____)

_____ MONEY MANAGEMENT/SAVINGS   (WHO? _____)

_____ CREDITORS/BANKRUPTCY   (WHO? _____)

_____ MENTAL ILLNESS   (WHO? _____)

_____ CRIME   (WHO? _____)

15. ARE YOUR CHILDREN WORKING?   _____ YES   _____ NO
IF YES, DESCRIBE EACH OF THEIR JOB(S). IF NO, EXPLAIN WHETHER
THEY ARE VOLUNTARILY NOT WORKING, LOOKING FOR WORK, OR DIS-
ABLED. _____
_____
_____
_____

16. IF ANY OF YOUR CHILDREN ARE DISABLED, LIST ANY DISABILITY
BENEFITS THEY ARE RECEIVING (E.G., SOCIAL SECURITY, SUPPLE-
MENTAL SECURITY INCOME, MEDICARE, MEDICAID, FOOD STAMPS,
SUBSIDIZED HOUSING, ETC.)

_____
_____
_____

17. HOW DO YOUR CHILDREN GET ALONG WITH ONE ANOTHER? DE-
SCRIBE ANY PROBLEM(S).

_____
_____
_____
_____
_____
_____

18. IF ANY OF YOUR CHILDREN ARE OR WILL BE UNABLE TO MANAGE FOR THEMSELVES, WHO IS CURRENTLY MANAGING FOR THEM, AND WHO SHOULD MANAGE FOR THEM AFTER YOU ARE GONE? IF YOUR FIRST CHOICE IS UNAVAILABLE, WHO ARE YOUR SECOND AND THIRD CHOICES? _____

_____

_____

19. DO YOU BELIEVE ANY OF YOUR CHILDREN MAY GET A DIVORCE?

_____

_____

20. DO YOU AND YOUR SPOUSE HAVE A PRENUPTIAL AGREEMENT?

_____

_____

21. IF YOU AND YOUR SPOUSE HAVE A PRENUPTIAL AGREEMENT, DO YOU STILL INTEND TO FOLLOW IT AND KEEP YOUR ASSETS SEPA-RATE? _____

_____

_____

22. AT YOUR DEATH, DO YOU WISH TO LEAVE EVERYTHING FOR YOUR SPOUSE? _____

_____

_____

23. HAS YOUR SPOUSE BEEN ACTIVELY INVOLVED IN MANAGING YOUR FAMILY'S FINANCES, AND WILL YOUR SPOUSE BE ABLE TO MANAGE AND HANDLE THE ASSETS AFTER YOUR DEATH? _____

_____

_____

_____

24. WHEN YOU AND YOUR SPOUSE ARE BOTH GONE, WHERE DO YOU WANT YOUR ASSETS TO GO AND IN WHAT AMOUNTS OR PROPORTIONS (E.G., DO YOU WANT TO LEAVE TO YOUR KIDS EQUAL OR UNEQUAL PORTIONS)? _____

_____

_____

_____

25. IF YOU LEAVE YOUR ASSETS TO YOUR SPOUSE, ARE YOU CONCERNED THAT YOUR SPOUSE MAY LATER LEAVE THE ASSETS TO A NEW SPOUSE OR PARTNER?_____

_____

_____

_____

26. HOW IMPORTANT IS IT TO LEAVE AS MUCH INHERITANCE AS POSSIBLE TO YOUR CHILDREN?

A. _____ VERY IMPORTANT

B. _____ MODERATELY IMPORTANT

C. _____ OKAY IF IT HAPPENS, BUT NOT A PRIORITY

D. _____ NOT IMPORTANT

E. _____ DEFINITELY DO *NOT* WANT TO LEAVE ANYTHING TO CHILDREN

27. HOW IMPORTANT IS IT TO YOU TO LEAVE SOMETHING TO CHARITY?

A. _____ VERY IMPORTANT

B. _____ MODERATELY IMPORTANT

C. _____ NOT IMPORTANT

28. WHICH CHARITY(IES) DO YOU WISH TO PROVIDE FOR AT YOUR DEATH? _____

_____

_____

_____

29. IF YOU BECOME UNABLE TO MANAGE YOUR FINANCES, WHO SHOULD TAKE OVER FOR YOU?

FIRST CHOICE: _____

SECOND CHOICE: _____

THIRD CHOICE: _____

30. IF YOU BECOME UNABLE TO MAKE YOUR OWN HEALTH CARE DE-CISIONS, WHO SHOULD MAKE THEM FOR YOU?

FIRST CHOICE: _____

SECOND CHOICE: _____

THIRD CHOICE: _____

31. DO YOU OWN A HOME?

A. _____   YES

B. _____   NO

32. IF SO, WHOSE NAME(S) IS IT IN?

_____

_____

33. WHAT IS THE:

A. APPRAISED VALUE OF THE HOME (FOR PROPERTY TAX PURPOSES)?
$

B. REAL MARKET VALUE IF YOU WERE TO SELL IT? $

34. IF YOU OWN OTHER REAL ESTATE:

A. WHOSE NAME(S) IS IT IN?

B. WHAT IS THE TAX APPRAISED VALUE? $

C. WHAT IS THE REAL MARKET VALUE? $

35. FOR EACH OF YOUR CHECKING ACCOUNTS, SAVINGS ACCOUNTS, CDS, AND MONEY MARKETS, LIST THE TYPE OF ACCOUNT, THE INSTI-

TUTION IT'S IN, THE OWNER(S) LISTED ON THE ACCOUNT, THE BENE-
FICIARY OF THE ACCOUNT, AND THE CURRENT DOLLAR VALUE.

	1.	2.
TYPE	_____	_____
INSTITUTION	_____	_____
OWNER(S)	_____	_____
BENEFICIARY(IES)	_____	_____
CURRENT VALUE	_____	_____

	3.	4.
TYPE	_____	_____
INSTITUTION	_____	_____
OWNER(S)	_____	_____
BENEFICIARY(IES)	_____	_____
CURRENT VALUE	_____	_____

	5.	6.
TYPE	_____	_____
INSTITUTION	_____	_____
OWNER(S)	_____	_____
BENEFICIARY(IES)	_____	_____
CURRENT VALUE	_____	_____

36. FOR STOCKS, BONDS, MUTUAL FUNDS, AND BROKERAGE AC-
COUNTS, LIST THE TYPE OF ASSET, THE INSTITUTION IT'S IN, THE
OWNER(S) OF THE ASSET, THE BENEFICIARY OF THE ASSET, THE
AMOUNT ORIGINALLY PAID, AND THE CURRENT MARKET VALUE.

	1.	2.
TYPE	_____	_____
INSTITUTION	_____	_____
OWNER(S)	_____	_____
BENEFICIARY(IES)	_____	_____
AMOUNT	_____	_____
CURRENT VALUE	_____	_____

	3.	4.
TYPE	_____	_____
INSTITUTION	_____	_____
OWNER(S)	_____	_____
BENEFICIARY(IES)	_____	_____
AMOUNT	_____	_____
CURRENT VALUE	_____	_____

	5.	6.
TYPE	_____	_____
INSTITUTION	_____	_____
OWNER(S)	_____	_____
BENEFICIARY(IES)	_____	_____
AMOUNT	_____	_____
CURRENT VALUE	_____	_____

37. FOR TAX-DEFERRED RETIREMENT ACCOUNTS, LIST THE TYPE (E.G., IRAS, 401(K)S, 403(B)S, PENSION AND PROFIT-SHARING PLANS, ETC.), THE INSTITUTION HOLDING THE ACCOUNT, THE OWNER OF THE ACCOUNT (I.E., YOU OR YOUR SPOUSE), THE BENEFICIARY(IES), AND THE CURRENT VALUE.

	1.	2.
TYPE	_____	_____
INSTITUTION	_____	_____
OWNER(S)	_____	_____
BENEFICIARY(IES)	_____	_____
CURRENT VALUE	_____	_____

	3.	4.
TYPE	_____	_____
INSTITUTION	_____	_____
OWNER(S)	_____	_____
BENEFICIARY(IES)	_____	_____
CURRENT VALUE	_____	_____

	5.	6.
TYPE	_____	_____
INSTITUTION	_____	_____
OWNER(S)	_____	_____
BENEFICIARY(IES)	_____	_____
CURRENT VALUE	_____	_____

38. IF YOU HAVE PURCHASED ANY ANNUITIES, LIST THE INSURANCE COMPANY, THE OWNER, THE BENEFICIARY(IES), THE YEAR PUR-CHASED, THE NUMBER OF YEARS LEFT WITH A SURRENDER PENALTY, THE CURRENT VALUE, AND ANY DEATH BENEFIT.

COMPANY	_____	_____
OWNER(S)	_____	_____
BENEFICIARY(IES)	_____	_____
YEAR	_____	_____
SURRENDER PENALTY	_____	_____
CURRENT VALUE	_____	_____
DEATH BENEFIT	_____	_____

39. FOR EACH LIFE INSURANCE POLICY, LIST THE COMPANY, THE OWNER, THE BENEFICIARY(IES), THE DEATH BENEFIT, AND THE CASH SURRENDER VALUE.

COMPANY	_____	_____
OWNER(S)	_____	_____
BENEFICIARY(IES)	_____	_____
DEATH BENEFIT	_____	_____
CASH VALUE	_____	_____

40. DO YOU OWN ANY LONG-TERM CARE INSURANCE? IF SO, LIST THE COMPANY, THE OWNER, THE NUMBER OF MONTHS/YEARS COV-ERED, THE PER DAY PAYMENT FOR NURSING HOME CARE, THE NA-TURE AND AMOUNT OF ANY OTHER CARE COVERED (E.G., ASSISTED

LIVING, HOME CARE), THE AMOUNT OF ANY INFLATION PROTECTION, AND THE PREMIUM.

COMPANY _____ _____

OWNER(S) _____ _____

MONTHS/YEARS
   COVERED _____ _____

PER DAY NURSING
   HOME PAYMENT _____ _____

OTHER CARE _____ _____

INFLATION
   PROTECTION _____ _____

PREMIUM _____ _____

41. IF YOU OWN AN INTEREST IN ANY BUSINESS, LIST THE TYPE (E.G., C CORPORATION, S CORPORATION, PARTNERSHIP, LIMITED LIA-BILITY COMPANY, SOLE PROPRIETORSHIP), YOUR PERCENTAGE OWN-ERSHIP, THE "COST BASIS" (GET FROM YOUR ACCOUNTANT), AND THE VALUE OF YOUR OWNERSHIP.

TYPE	PERCENTAGE	COST BASIS	VALUE
_____	_____	_____	_____
_____	_____	_____	_____
_____	_____	_____	_____
_____	_____	_____	_____
_____	_____	_____	_____
_____	_____	_____	_____
_____	_____	_____	_____
_____	_____	_____	_____
_____	_____	_____	_____
_____	_____	_____	_____
_____	_____	_____	_____
_____	_____	_____	_____
_____	_____	_____	_____

42. FOR EACH CAR YOU OWN, LIST THE OWNER(S), THE MAKE, MODEL, AND YEAR, AND THE APPROXIMATE MARKET VALUE.

OWNER(S)	MAKE, MODEL AND YEAR	VALUE
_____	_____	_____
_____	_____	_____
_____	_____	_____
_____	_____	_____
_____	_____	_____
_____	_____	_____

43. IF YOU HAVE ANY PERSONAL ITEMS WITH SIGNIFICANT VALUE (MORE THAN $1,000), LIST THE OWNER(S), ASSET TYPE (E.G., JEWELRY, COINS, STAMP AND GUN COLLECTION, ART, ETC.), AND THE APPROXIMATE MARKET VALUE.

OWNER(S)	ASSET TYPE	VALUE
_____	_____	_____
_____	_____	_____
_____	_____	_____
_____	_____	_____
_____	_____	_____
_____	_____	_____

44. FOR ANY DEBTS/LOANS, LIST THE DEBTOR(S), NATURE OF THE DEBT (E.G., MORTGAGE, HOME EQUITY, CAR LOAN, TAXES, FAMILY LOAN), THE APPROXIMATE BALANCE, AND ANY PAYOFF DATE.

DEBTOR(S)	NATURE	BALANCE	PAYOFF DATE
_____	_____	_____	_____
_____	_____	_____	_____
_____	_____	_____	_____
_____	_____	_____	_____

_____   _____   _____   _____
_____   _____   _____   _____
_____   _____   _____   _____

45. FOR ANY REGULAR, FIXED INCOME PAYMENTS, LIST THE RECIPI-
ENT, NATURE (E.G., SOCIAL SECURITY, PENSION, ANNUITY, ETC.),
AND AMOUNT.

RECIPIENT	NATURE	AMOUNT
_____	_____	_____
_____	_____	_____
_____	_____	_____
_____	_____	_____
_____	_____	_____
_____	_____	_____

46. HOW MUCH ARE YOU TAKING FROM YOUR RETIREMENT FUNDS—
IRAS, 401(K)S, ETC.—EACH YEAR? _____
_____

47. ABOUT HOW MUCH IN INTEREST, DIVIDENDS, RENTS, AND WAGES
(IF WORKING) DO YOU RECEIVE? _____
_____

48. HOW MUCH ARE YOUR MONTHLY EXPENSES?
RENT/MORTGAGE: _____
UTILITIES (HEAT, WATER, ELECTRIC): _____
PROPERTY TAXES: _____
HOMEOWNERS INSURANCE: _____
FOOD: _____
CLOTHING: _____
CAR (GAS AND MAINTENANCE): _____
HEALTH INSURANCE: _____
ADDITIONAL HEALTH COSTS: _____

CAREGIVERS: _____

TRAVEL: _____

ENTERTAINMENT: _____

PUBLICATIONS (MAGAZINES, NEWSPAPERS): _____

DEBT/LOAN PAYMENTS: _____

EDUCATION: _____

SUPPORT FOR OTHERS: _____

CHARITABLE CONTRIBUTIONS: _____

OTHER: _____

TOTAL _____

49. FOR ANY GIFTS OF MORE THAN $500 MADE DURING THE LAST FIVE YEARS, LIST THE RECIPIENT, DATE, PURPOSE (E.G., BIRTHDAY, WEDDING, TAX PLANNING, MEDICAID PLANNING), AND AMOUNT, AND STATE WHETHER ANY GIFT TAX RETURN WAS FILED.

	1.	2.
RECIPIENT	_____	_____
DATE	_____	_____
PURPOSE	_____	_____
AMOUNT	_____	_____
GIFT TAX RETURN	_____	_____

	3.	4.
RECIPIENT	_____	_____
DATE	_____	_____
PURPOSE	_____	_____
AMOUNT	_____	_____
GIFT TAX RETURN	_____	_____

	5.	6.
RECIPIENT	_____	_____
DATE	_____	_____
PURPOSE	_____	_____

AMOUNT _____ _____

GIFT TAX RETURN _____ _____

50. WHAT ARE YOUR MOST IMPORTANT ESTATE-PLANNING GOALS?
TAKE YOUR TIME, RANK IN ORDER FROM 1 TO 16.

_____ AVOID PROBATE.

_____ CUT TAXES.

_____ PROTECT ASSETS FROM NURSING HOME COSTS.

_____ PRESERVE ESTATE FOR CHILDREN.

_____ PRESERVE ESTATE FOR GRANDCHILDREN.

_____ LEAVE ASSETS TO CHARITY.

_____ PROTECT ASSETS FROM CHILDREN'S SPOUSES.

_____ ASSURE GRANDCHILDREN RECEIVE REMAINING ESTATE AFTER
YOUR CHILDREN PASS ON.

_____ PROTECT LOVED ONE WITH A DISABILITY.

_____ MAXIMIZE ESTATE PRESERVATION PRIMARILY FOR SPOUSE.

_____ PRESERVE ESTATE FOR BOTH SPOUSE AND CHILDREN.

_____ PROTECT ASSETS FROM CHILDREN'S LAWSUITS/CREDITORS.

_____ MAKE SURE SOMEONE CAN MANAGE YOUR FINANCES IF YOU'RE
DISABLED.

_____ ENSURE NO HEROIC MEASURES ARE TAKEN TO KEEP YOU ALIVE.

_____ MAKE SURE SOMEONE CAN MAKE YOUR HEALTH DECISIONS IF
YOU CAN'T.

_____ OTHER

Congratulations, you've successfully completed your SAT! Now let's briefly discuss its significance. This is only an overview; the real importance of these questions and your answers will become readily apparent when you read the rest of this book.

The SAFE Assessment Tool is divided into ten general categories:

- Preliminary personal information (#1–5)
- Health information (#6–8)
- Children and in-laws (#9–19)
- Intended heirs at death (#20–28)
- Asset management during life (#29–30)
- Assets/Debts (#31–44)
- Income (#45–47)
- Expenses (#48)
- Gifts (#49)
- Planning goals (#50)

The importance of information about your age and marital status is probably obvious. But why is your and your spouse's health relevant to estate planning? Isn't estate planning about your money and property? Unfortunately, your and your spouse's health may have a huge impact on your finances, and, therefore, on your planning. For example, if your spouse has just been diagnosed with Alzheimer's disease, preparing Financial Durable Powers of Attorney and Health Care Durable Powers of Attorney is essential, so you will be able to handle the family finances and make health care decisions as circumstances change. And you may need to adopt a plan to protect assets if expensive nursing home care for either one of you becomes necessary.

Much of estate planning involves planning for your heirs after you're gone. For example, avoiding probate and taxes at your death won't help *you*, but it will make life easier for your heirs and save them money after you're gone. When setting your estate plan, the personal, marital, and financial situations of your children *must* be considered, and that's why questions 9–19 are important. You should consider how you want to distribute your estate. Just because you have kids doesn't mean you have to leave them anything, and your children do not have to be treated equally. For example, you may choose to leave more to your single son who works as a teacher than to your high-powered lawyer daughter married to a high-powered doctor. Maybe you will wish to use a SAFE Trust to provide work incentives for a child who is chronically lazy, or you might want to set up a SAFE Trust to protect the inheritance for your daughter who's married to a bum. If charitable gifting is important to you, a good SAFE plan may enable you to maximize the benefits. And leaving assets directly to a child who is disabled could create more problems than it solves.

Many people today are concerned about the inheritance intended for children and grandchildren winding up with the in-laws. That's why it's important to ascertain information about your children's spouses or significant others.

Knowing the relationship between you and your spouse, and between your spouse and your children, often plays a role in a SAFE plan. For example, leaving assets to a spouse who is not the parent of your kids, and who does not have a good relationship with your offspring, may mean your kids will wind up with nothing. The answers to questions 20–22 of your SAT may lead you to set up a SAFE Trust that benefits your spouse during his/her life while also protecting an inheritance for your children.

Not all estate planning is planning for your estate after your death. What if you were to become incapacitated during your life? Who should manage and make decisions for you? When you die, will your spouse be capable of managing the finances, or should you build assistance into your SAFE plan? These questions are often overlooked but play an important part in establishing a good estate plan.

Many of the questions in the SAFE Assessment Tool (beginning with question 31) address your assets. Much more information than just the total amount or value of the asset is needed. The home is most people's biggest asset, and it may get special protection from creditors, nursing home costs, and taxes, but that may depend on how it is titled. For most assets that have gone up in value over time (e.g., real estate and stocks), you'll pay capital gains tax on any profit made when you sell them. If you give appreciated assets to children or other family members during your lifetime, they'll pay tax when the assets are sold. But if you leave them to heirs at death, they'll generally pay *no* capital gains tax. So when developing a SAFE plan, understanding the purchase price and market value of your assets is important.

The tax status of your investments also is critical information. For example, as you remove funds from tax-deferred retirement accounts such as IRAs or annuities, you'll pay income tax. If you remove funds from annuities within a set number of years after the purchase (usually seven to ten years), you'll pay a penalty on top of the taxes. With proper planning, your heirs may get special income tax breaks on these assets after you pass away.

Beneficiary designations on assets, including insurance, IRAs, and annuities, play an important role in your SAFE planning. For example, naming your spouse or child as beneficiary may undermine your wishes for your family, while naming a SAFE Trust may provide special protections.

Life insurance and long-term care insurance can provide special protections for you and your family, and these policies allow some valuable planning opportunities.

The questions concerning your debts and expenses are critical for determining how much money (if any) you'll have left, after your normal expenses, for savings, gifting, or other planning. And many people are surprised to learn they're actually spending *more* than their current income, a possible prescription for disaster.

The last question, "What are your most important estate-planning goals," is the most important. For example, your best plan to avoid probate or cut taxes may be the worst approach to take if you wish to protect your savings from nursing home costs. With proper, comprehensive, SAFE planning, you will stack the deck in your favor for achieving your most important desires.

As you read through the rest of this book, refer back to your answers to the SAT questions. Don't worry, it's okay to change answers as you go. The SAT is designed to help you organize your thoughts and develop your plans for your and your family's future.

CHAPTER 3

The Three
Most Important
SAFE Protections

Take a look at your answers to the SAT. What are your major concerns and goals, and the major risks to your family? If you are like most people, in addition to probate avoidance (which a standard Revocable Living Trust can achieve), you'd like to accomplish three important goals:

- *Protecting your child's inheritance in a divorce.* An inheritance left to a child often becomes "marital" over time, which means that the spouse will become entitled to a portion in a divorce. With proper planning, you can keep the inheritance insulated from your child's spouse.

- *Protecting your grandchildren's inheritance at your child's death.* Your married child will probably leave everything to the spouse, including any inheritance received from you. And once it's in the spouse's account, you have no say. But with planning that looks into the future, you can guarantee that your grandchildren will receive your inheritance after your children pass on.

- *Protecting your family from creditors and lawsuits.* We live in a litigious society; people sue for all sorts of things. If your child is successfully sued after receiving an inheritance, those funds could be grabbed. But an inheritance can be protected if you use a SAFE plan.

Whether you leave your assets to heirs under a will, or by naming joint owners, or by designating beneficiaries, or by creating a standard Revocable Living Trust, the bottom line is always the same: your heirs get the inheritance outright and directly. Your money and property become theirs. If your child later gets a divorce, the former spouse may wind up with half of the inheritance meant for your child; if your child dies after receiving the inheritance, *all* your money is likely to go to the child's spouse; and if your child later gets sued, your money may go to pay your child's creditors. The only way you can avoid having your family bled dry by these family disasters is by utilizing a SAFE estate plan.

You would start with a Starter Trust, typically the Revocable Living Trust, putting your money and property in during your life. At your death, the trust will avoid probate, automatically passing your assets into a SAFE Trust for each of your children.

Consider this example.

Jane's SAFE Trust

Jane sets up a standard Revocable Living Trust for herself. During her lifetime, Jane is her own trustee. She keeps control over her investments and can remove any money for herself whenever she wishes. At her death, she wants to avoid probate and to leave everything to her two children, Bob and Mary. But she wants her inheritance to stay with her children and not to go to their spouses or creditors. So she combines the Revocable Living Trust with SAFE Trusts for her children. Instead of Bob and Mary inheriting outright, at Jane's death half the inheritance is automatically placed into a SAFE Trust for Bob and the other half goes into a SAFE Trust for Mary.

Bob and Mary are both responsible adults who can manage money, so Jane has named them as their own trustees of their SAFE Trusts: Bob as his trustee, Mary as hers. That's the way most folks do it. Bob will be in charge of his own trust, Mary in charge of hers, just as Jane is in charge of the Revocable Living Trust while she's alive.

After Jane's gone, her children will manage their individual SAFE Trusts. They can decide how to invest the funds in their own SAFE Trusts. Stocks, bonds, CDs, real estate—each child can invest as he or she sees fit.

And Jane's children can take money out of their SAFE Trusts for anything they need. "Needs" are defined broadly and generally include food, clothing, shelter (rent or mortgage payments, or money to buy a home), transportation, health care, entertainment, travel, and education. For example, if Bob wants to use his SAFE Trust to pay for a new suit, or his health insurance premium, no problem. Bob just takes the money out. He doesn't have to ask anyone's permission. If Mary wants to use the funds in her SAFE Trust to pay her children's college tuition and room and board, that's okay too. Jane set up the SAFE Trust to allow Bob and Mary to make their own decisions.

JANE'S REVOCABLE LIVING TRUST WITH SAFE TRUSTS FOR HER CHILDREN

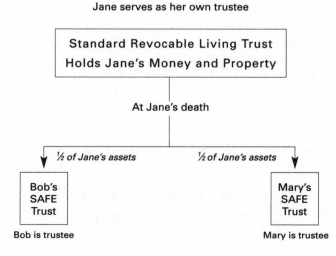

Jane serves as her own trustee

Standard Revocable Living Trust
Holds Jane's Money and Property

At Jane's death

½ of Jane's assets   ½ of Jane's assets

Bob's SAFE Trust   Mary's SAFE Trust

Bob is trustee   Mary is trustee

So where's the benefit? If your kids can manage the funds and use them for their needs, how does that differ from just leaving the inheritance outright to them? That's where the SAFE plan comes in.

SAFE Benefit 1: Divorce Protection

If your child gets a divorce, the SAFE Trust protects the assets that remain in the trust and have not yet been spent. Let's look at a real case:

The Case of Louise

Louise received an inheritance of $150,000 at her mother Rita's death. Instead of leaving it outright, the inheritance was passed to Louise in a SAFE Trust. Louise served as her own trustee, and over the years chose to spend the interest generated by her investments. But she didn't touch the principal, which was invested in mutual funds at a brokerage firm.

Ten years after her mother died, Louise was surprised when her husband Jack announced he wanted a divorce. Now you'll see how the benefits

LOUISE AND JACK'S DIVORCE
DIVISION OF THEIR OWN MARITAL ASSETS

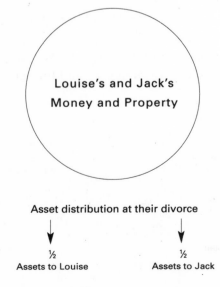

Louise's and Jack's
Money and Property

Asset distribution at their divorce

½
Assets to Louise

½
Assets to Jack

of the SAFE Trust create a safety net: in general, all of the marital assets were split, half to Louise, half to her husband.

It made no difference whose name the assets were in: husband, wife, or joint. The judge threw everything into one pot and split it down the middle.

With one major exception: the $150,000 remaining in the SAFE Trust. Those assets were safe—they belonged entirely to Louise. Her husband Jack was not entitled to one penny of Louise's SAFE Trust. The SAFE Trust could not be considered part of the couple's "split-able" joint married assets. Jack could make no legitimate claim.

The SAFE Trust withstood Jack's attack.

RITA'S REVOCABLE LIVING TRUST WITH A SAFE TRUST FOR HER DAUGHTER

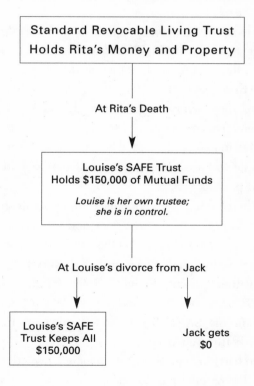

Bottom Line: The SAFE Trust protects assets during a divorce.

How did this work? The domestic relations judge handling the divorce explained that only marital assets are split in a divorce. Marital assets are assets generated by the couple during the marriage. Inheritances generally start out as separate assets, not marital assets. But over time, couples often commingle their resources, sharing income and expenses, and treating the assets as "theirs." The separate nature of the inheritance then may disappear. An inheritance left in a SAFE Trust maintains its separate nature, and maintains its protection from the spouse in a divorce.

SAFE Benefit 2: Protection at Child's Death

The SAFE Trust protects an inheritance for your blood or adopted family (or other chosen heirs) and keeps it from passing to your child's spouse at your child's death. Let's look at another real-life case.

The Case of Richard

Richard's estate was set up like most people's: he and his wife Sherry were leaving everything to each other. When one died, the other would get everything. Their wills went on to state that, at the second death, their assets would pass to their children.

When Richard died, everything he owned, and everything he and Sherry jointly owned, passed as planned to Sherry. Years later, Sherry met a new guy, Steve, fell in love, and decided to remarry. At Sherry's death, she left her entire estate to Steve. Her children, Richard's children, received nothing from their parents' estate.

Fortunately, there's a happier economic ending to this story. Richard's parents, Sally and Tom, had taken my advice and set up a SAFE Trust. If the inheritance had gone to Richard directly, it would have ended up in the hands of Sherry's new husband, Steve, just like everything else Richard owned. Instead, at their passing, Richard's $200,000 inheritance was distributed to a SAFE Trust for his use and benefit. When Richard died, the assets remaining in his SAFE Trust passed pursuant to his parent's wishes—to Richard's three children.

While Richard had left everything he *personally* owned to his wife, the inheritance from his parents passed according to *their* wishes, to their grandchildren. Thanks to their SAFE plan, Richard's children received an

RICHARD'S PERSONAL ASSETS
(NO SAFE TRUST)

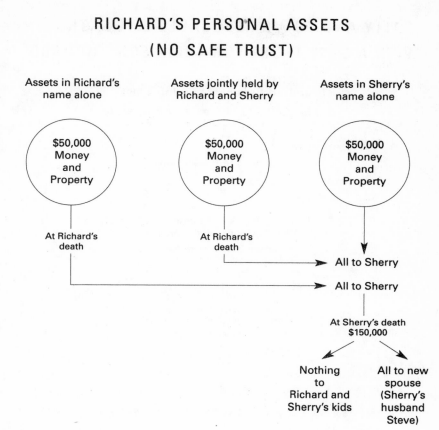

Assets in Richard's name alone

Assets jointly held by Richard and Sherry

Assets in Sherry's name alone

$50,000 Money and Property

$50,000 Money and Property

$50,000 Money and Property

At Richard's death

At Richard's death

All to Sherry

All to Sherry

At Sherry's death
$150,000

Nothing to Richard and Sherry's kids

All to new spouse (Sherry's husband Steve)

inheritance. If not for the SAFE Trust, the estate of Richard's parents would have passed from Richard to Sherry to her new husband, and completely out of the family.

What if your child does not have children? What would then happen when your child dies? Not to worry. The remaining assets in your child's SAFE Trust would pass to whomever *you* designate in the trust (unless you voluntarily give your children the power to designate heirs). Most people pass their assets to their other surviving children or grandchildren. Or the remaining funds could pass to your child's spouse (if that's *your* choice). And some people designate their favorite charities to be the ultimate recipient of anything that remains. Let's take a look at another real situation.

SALLY AND TOM'S REVOCABLE LIVING TRUST WITH A SAFE TRUST FOR THEIR SON, RICHARD

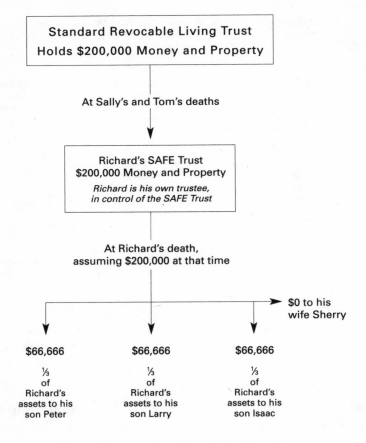

Standard Revocable Living Trust
Holds $200,000 Money and Property

At Sally's and Tom's deaths

Richard's SAFE Trust
$200,000 Money and Property
*Richard is his own trustee,
in control of the SAFE Trust*

At Richard's death,
assuming $200,000 at that time

$0 to his
wife Sherry

$66,666

⅓
of
Richard's
assets to his
son Peter

$66,666

⅓
of
Richard's
assets to his
son Larry

$66,666

⅓
of
Richard's
assets to his
son Isaac

Bottom Line: SAFE Trust protects the grandchildren.

The Case of Rose Ann

Rose Ann had three wonderful children. To protect them, and her blood family, she established SAFE Trusts for them. At Rose Ann's death, one-third of her estate passed to the SAFE Trusts for each of her kids. Under the terms of their SAFE Trusts, Randi, Lisa, and Sandy each managed their trust funds, taking money whenever they needed something.

About ten years after Rose Ann died, her daughter Randi passed on. Randi was married but had no children. Randi left her own home, IRA, bank accounts, and other assets that she had earned to her husband. And that was just fine.

But Rose Ann wanted her children and grandchildren, not their spouses, to benefit from her inheritance. So she set up the children's SAFE Trusts to pass at their deaths to their children, if they had any. Lisa and Sandy had children, and their shares were set to pass on to their kids. But

ROSE ANN'S REVOCABLE LIVING TRUST
WITH SAFE TRUSTS FOR HER CHILDREN

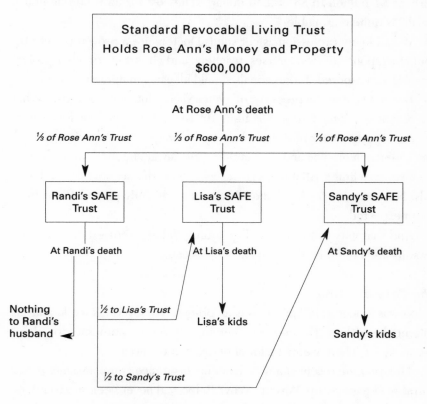

Bottom Line: SAFE Trust assets can go to your other children instead of to "non-SAFE" parties (e.g., child's spouse).

Randi was childless. At her death, the remainder in her trust passed into her sisters' SAFE Trusts, just as Rose Ann had planned.

SAFE Benefit 3: Lawsuit and Creditor Protection

It's sad but true, we live in a litigious society. Lawsuits could almost qualify as a national hobby. Today people sue for all sorts of reasons. Some lawsuits are well founded, others are not. Some plaintiffs lose, some win. But if you or your children are successfully sued, all your assets could be taken.

Everyone should have insurance to protect against liability. As a motorist, you must have auto liability insurance. As a homeowner, you must have homeowner's liability insurance. And you should probably consider getting an umbrella policy with higher liability coverage than is "standard," perhaps $1 million to $5 million dollars. The cost for an umbrella policy usually is quite reasonable.

We all know professionals get sued. Doctors are a proven target. Accountants, police officers, nurses, teachers, and almost every other professional is also exposed. Professionals should all carry malpractice coverage.

If you own a rental property, or even a vacant lot, you are at risk. What if a tenant or visitor falls and is injured? You guessed it—you'll be sued! Every property owner must have liability coverage.

Unfortunately, you and your children can always be sued for more than the insurance limits. All it takes is one collision with a school bus filled with kids. No one can *ever* have enough insurance to fully protect them from the unexpected.

And that gets us to the SAFE planning to keep your estate safe from lawsuits and creditors. Let's look at Ralph's case.

The Case of Ralph

Ralph was a doctor; in fact, he was an ob-gyn. He loved his work, and his patients loved him. He had been serving his rural community for about twenty years. There weren't a lot of ob-gyns in the area.

This year, he received a note from his insurance company stating that his rates were going up. Way up. Why? Ralph had never been sued, and the insurance company had never had to pay out a dime on a claim against him. But that didn't stop the rate hike.

Ralph maintained a decent level of coverage, but he couldn't afford to increase the limits. He understood that if anyone ever did recover a judgment against him for more than the insurance limits, he could lose everything.

Well, not everything. Ralph was comforted in knowing that when his parents had died, they had left his inheritance in a SAFE Trust for him. This was designed to protect the funds from creditors and lawsuits. He could use the funds as he needed them, but these funds would be protected if he should be sued. This peace of mind, knowing that a lawsuit couldn't wipe him out entirely, made it possible for him to continue practicing medicine.

The SAFE Trust (attached to a Revocable Living Trust) can be used to protect your *children's* inheritance from lawsuits and creditors, after you're gone. But this does not insulate *you* from lawsuit and creditor attacks while you're alive. To protect *yourself*, you'll need to consider another Starter Trust, called a Creditor Protection Trust (Chapter 6). And if you wish to continue the creditor and lawsuit protections for the lives of your

LEN AND RUTH'S REVOCABLE LIVING TRUST WITH A SAFE TRUST FOR THEIR SON RALPH

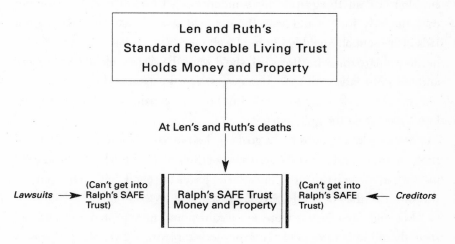

Bottom Line: SAFE Trust is protected from lawsuits and creditors.

grandchildren, and possibly longer, you'll need to create a Dynasty SAFE Trust (discussed later in this chapter).

The SAFE Trust protections, to safeguard the children's inheritances in case of a divorce, death, or lawsuit, are extremely valuable. And the *only* way to get all these wonderful benefits is with a SAFE Trust.

Does it matter how much your estate is worth? Must you have a large estate to go into a SAFE Trust? The answer is no. SAFE Trusts have provided tremendous protections for folks with millions of dollars, *and* for people with very modest estates. You *don't* have to be rich to create a SAFE Trust. Let me tell you the story of my clients, Mr. and Mrs. Jacobs.

The Jacobses' Story

Mr. and Mrs. Jacobs were not wealthy. They owned their home, valued at about $150,000. And they had savings of no more than $50,000.

Their daughter, Jody, and Jody's three kids were the apples of their eyes. They loved Jody and had an extremely warm relationship with Jody's children, their grandchildren. The only dark spot in their family portrait was their son-in-law, Seth. Jody saw something in him that her parents could not. In their eyes, he was a bum. He refused to get a job, insisting he couldn't find anything up to his standards. That forced Jody to work *and* raise the kids. Jody would leave the house at about 8 A.M., after seeing her kids off to school. She'd get home by about 5:30 P.M. Then it was time for her to prepare dinner. Afterward, she'd wash the dishes, clean the kitchen, and help her kids with their homework. Her husband? He spent his day out, supposedly looking for work. But how much work could he find at the local bar? Or on the golf course?

Mr. and Mrs. Jacobs had a goal for their estate plan: to leave assets for their daughter and her children, to make their lives a little better. And *most* important, to keep the inheritance from Jody's husband, Seth. The solution was obvious: they needed a SAFE Trust.

Mr. and Mrs. Jacobs were not wealthy, and they probably would not (and should not) have paid the expense for a trust if the *only* goal was to avoid probate. Creating a basic Revocable Living Trust might cost $1,500

MR. AND MRS. JACOBS'S REVOCABLE
LIVING TRUST WITH A SAFE TRUST
FOR THEIR DAUGHTER JODY

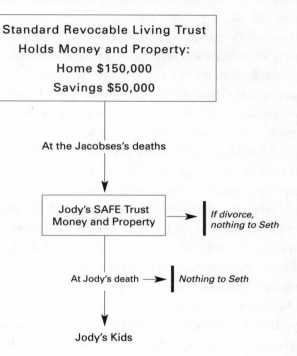

Standard Revocable Living Trust
Holds Money and Property:
Home $150,000
Savings $50,000

At the Jacobses's deaths

Jody's SAFE Trust
Money and Property

If divorce,
nothing to Seth

At Jody's death → Nothing to Seth

Jody's Kids

**Bottom Line: SAFE Trust keeps inheritance for
children and grandchildren, and away from unsafe spouses.**

to $3,000. They could have easily and inexpensively accomplished the goal
of probate avoidance simply by naming Jody as beneficiary on their home
and CDs. But that would not have protected the inheritance from Seth.

Even though a SAFE Trust is much more costly than naming beneficiaries, and even more expensive than using a Revocable Living Trust alone,
it is also *much* more protective. And for Mr. and Mrs. Jacobs, the added
cost was well worth it. (The costs are discussed in Chapter 10.)

Some people ask me: Why not just leave my assets outright to my children, and let *them* make their own estate plans, which would provide these same benefits? The problem is that they *can't* get the same benefits themselves. In general, the laws permit *you* to protect an inheritance for your children much more easily and more fully than they could ever accomplish for themselves.

Let's take lawsuits and creditors. A person cannot easily protect his own assets from lawsuits and creditors. Sure, a person could take extreme steps, like putting his funds in an offshore trust, giving up control to some independent trustee located in the Cayman or Cook Islands. But the law makes it much easier and more favorable for a *parent* to provide lawsuit and creditor protections for the inheritance left to the kids in a SAFE Trust.

And the same holds for the divorce and death protections. Your children could protect their assets from their spouses by making prenuptial agreements, but how many actually do that? Not many! When people marry, they often have stars in their eyes and blinders over their hearts. Even in second or third marriages, when most folks should know better, few people protect themselves with prenuptial arrangements. In the real world, it's far more practical for parents to create protections for their children's inheritances, by creating SAFE Trusts.

As you can see, the benefits of SAFE planning and SAFE Trusts can be wonderful. There's no other way to protect your family from spouses in a divorce or at death, and from creditors and lawsuits. But the question I often get is: Do SAFE Trusts really work?

While laws can change, the answer right now is a resounding "Yes." Except in rare circumstances, SAFE Trusts protect your family. What are the key exceptions? The IRS may be able to crack a SAFE Trust. Some states allow a person seeking court-ordered child or spousal support to break into a SAFE Trust, and some states allow creditors that provided critical services to an individual to collect reimbursement from a SAFE Trust. For example, if a shelter provides food needed to save your son's life, it may be able to collect reimbursement from a SAFE Trust. And a couple of states (Georgia and Oklahoma) allow victims of intentional torts (such as assaults) to go after SAFE Trusts. But this exception is extremely limited.

How strong is a SAFE Trust? Let's take a look at a couple of extreme cases. In the case of *Scheffel v. Krueger*, Lorie Scheffel sued Kyle Krueger for sexually assaulting her young child, videotaping the act, then broadcasting it on the Internet. The New Hampshire Supreme Court entered a default judgment against Krueger for $551,000.

Krueger's grandmother years earlier had created a trust for Krueger with SAFE provisions. The New Hampshire Supreme Court ruled that the trust was shielded and could not be touched by Scheffel.

In another case, James Calvert McGee was convicted of killing Katherine Ryon. Her estate sued, and the parties agreed to entry of judgment in the total amount of $600,000. McGee was the beneficiary of a trust, established by his mother, containing more than $800,000. The Maryland Court of Appeals ruled in 2003 that the trust assets, which were protected by SAFE provisions, could not be reached to satisfy the judgment.

It should be easy to see that a trust that is strong enough to shelter assets from the victim of a sexual assault or a murder is certainly capable of insulating funds from your child's spouse or financial creditors. States are free to create exceptions to the SAFE Trust protections; so far, very few have chosen to do so.

For a SAFE Trust to insulate your child's inheritance from lawsuits and creditors, in some states your child will have to step down as trustee and turn control over to another. This is often called a "spendthrift" provision.

As we've explained, SAFE Trusts can help you accomplish three important goals: protect your child's inheritance in a divorce, protect your grandchildren's inheritance at your child's death, and protect your children and grandchildren from creditors and lawsuits. But there's more, lots more. These same benefits can be extended for future generations, they can be extended to nonfamily members, they can be used to protect gifts to your children during your lifetime (not just after you die), and they can preserve your family's privacy. Take a look at SAFE Benefits 4 to 7 below.

SAFE Benefit 4: Privacy Protection.

In addition to protecting your life savings from your children's spouses, lawsuits, and creditors, there's a fourth basic benefit for you and your family from a SAFE Trust: *privacy*. Most people don't focus on this issue. But it's important and should not be overlooked.

Anyone who values privacy dreads probate, because, in most states, during probate your entire estate becomes public record: an open book for any nosy relative, nasty neighbor, or aggressive telemarketer, salesman, or con man. This happens because the probate court requires that everything you own must be itemized, listed, and disclosed.

How much did you keep in the bank? It's an open record. Did you own stocks and bonds? Again, it's readily available. What's the value of your car, jewelry, and household furnishings? Might as well hang out a sign: Come and look. Did you own a home? It's right there in the court papers.

Not only are your assets an open book, but your will is too. Did you leave more to one relative than another? They'll have a right to see exactly what you did by examining the will. If you think you can outsmart the system simply by not leaving a will, think again. You'll be worse off, because not only will your estate still go through probate, but also the state now will decide who gets your money!

In these days of sophisticated scams and con artists looking for any possible angle, you're opening your family up to hassles and headaches when your assets go through probate. For example, con artists might send false bills to your family, claiming that you had hired them to paint the house or provide home care, and you never paid. When you're dead, who can disprove the claim? Your children may go ahead and pay, falling prey to a common scheme.

Scam artists will also see the names of your beneficiaries and the amounts of their inheritance. For a con man, this is like a gift from heaven (presumably that's where you'll be!).

Avoiding probate keeps your estate private. A Revocable Living Trust enables you to bypass probate, assuring that at your death there's no information available to con artists looking to make a score. Your assets pass to the children or other heirs with no public record. But we're not done yet. A Revocable Living Trust is not sufficient to totally insulate your estate from unintended eyes. There's one more step you'll want to take and that's to combine your Revocable Living Trust with a SAFE Trust for the family.

By passing your estate into SAFE Trusts for the children, you keep the inheritance private so that your child's spouse will have no right to know about the inheritance. It might sound like tough love, but you'll quickly see it's a very loving action. Let's say your child's spouse files for divorce after you're gone. The spouse would probably know about any inheritance left outright to your child. And even if the child's spouse didn't know *before* the divorce, he or she almost certainly would be able to force your child as part of the divorce proceedings to disclose the inheritance. But by passing the inheritance into a SAFE Trust, you ensure that your child has a shield against disclosure.

When your child dies, the child's spouse normally would have a right to know of any asset in your child's name, including any of the inheritance left outright to the child. In fact, the spouse may have a right to take a portion of the child's estate under state law. But if the inheritance is in a SAFE Trust, not only does the spouse have no rights to the assets, the spouse has no right to even know about the assets in the SAFE Trust.

The privacy of a SAFE Trust even helps if your child is sued. A SAFE Trust will make it tougher for a creditor to find out that your child has even received any inheritance. And depending on the terms of the SAFE Trust and the laws of your state, the creditor may be prevented from learning the amount of assets in the SAFE Trust and the terms of the SAFE Trust. The more roadblocks that you can put between your child and the child's creditors, the better for your child.

There is one exception to the complete privacy provided by a SAFE Trust, and that exception is your home. You'll have to put the home into the name of your Revocable Living Trust to have it avoid probate. And while there's no record in probate court, the deed putting the home into the trust must be filed as a public record in the local office of the recorder of deeds. This isn't so terrible. The only information anyone could pick up is that a trust exists with a home in it. There will be no information about the terms or beneficiaries of the trust, or the nature and value of your other assets. Once you die and the home is sold, that's it. The proceeds will be paid into the name of *your* trust, which will then allocate the money into the SAFE Trusts for the children—with no public record whatsoever.

But if you don't even wish to have the existence of your trust anywhere noted in any public record, you could purchase or put the home in the name of a limited liability company, which can have a name unconnected to your family name (for example, the "XYZ Company"), and then have the ownership of the company placed into your trust. Then there would be *no* public record of your trust at all. See Chapter 6 for more information about a limited liability company.

Most people focus on trusts to avoid the costs and hassles of probate. And the most talked-about benefits of SAFE Trusts are the protections for your children from their spouses and lawsuits. But in these days, when our personal information seems vulnerable from so many fronts, don't overlook the tremendous benefit that SAFE Trusts provide to build the walls of privacy around your assets and your children's inheritances.

SAFE Benefit 5: Extension Protection for Future Generations

In our discussions so far, the SAFE Trust protections lasted for one generation. That satisfies most folks. Your kids' inheritances avoid probate, are kept confidential, and are protected for the blood family in the event of divorce, death, and lawsuits. But when your children die, the inheritance passes outright and unprotected to their children, or whomever you have set forth as the beneficiaries. That's the end of the line. The grandchildren get the inheritance, and it's theirs to spend and to lose.

In a typical SAFE Trust, you'd provide for supervision for the grandchildren's inheritance if they're youngsters. For example, you'd typically keep the inheritance in a SAFE Trust for their benefit until they reach age twenty-five, or thirty, or whatever age you decide is appropriate. But at some point the SAFE Trust ends and the funds become theirs with no strings attached.

If your grandchild gets divorced, there's no protection; the spouse will go after half. If your grandchild dies, there's no protection. In all likelihood the assets get left to the spouse, who may later leave it to some other person, maybe a new spouse, outside of your blood family. If your grandchild is sued, there's no protection.

If those scenarios don't appeal to you, and if you wish to extend the SAFE Trust protections beyond one generation, guess what? You can! It's called a Dynasty SAFE Trust.

A Dynasty SAFE Trust provides the SAFE protections for your family for more than one generation—and in some states *forever!* You can protect the inheritance you leave, not only for your children's lives but also for the lives of your grandchildren, and possibly great-grandchildren, great-great-grandchildren, and on and on. If *any* of them gets a divorce, the inheritance in the SAFE Trust is protected from that person's spouse. When they die, the remaining assets go down the family line—to their children, not to the spouses. (If a person dies with no children, the inheritance can go to the deceased person's closest blood relatives, typically his or her siblings, nephews, or nieces). The SAFE Trust assets are protected from lawsuits for multiple generations.

How does the Dynasty SAFE Trust work? At your death, the inheritance you're leaving passes into SAFE Trusts for each of your children, just as described before. Your children can manage those funds, and take money out as needed.

But when your child dies, the remaining assets pass automatically into Dynasty SAFE Trusts for your child's children (or, if no kids, into Dynasty SAFE Trusts for your other children or grandchildren). So, for example, when you die, the inheritance goes into a SAFE Trust for your son. When your son dies, the remaining assets may go into a Dynasty SAFE Trust for his children. When they die, the remaining assets may go into Dynasty SAFE Trusts for their children if the trusts and state law allow. The protections may go on and on, until all the funds are used up. Take a look at William's story to see how this worked.

The Story of William

William loved the protections offered by SAFE Trusts. But he didn't want to provide those benefits only for his children. His choice was to give his descendants the opportunity to benefit from his estate for as long as the money held out.

So William created Dynasty SAFE Trusts for his heirs. At William's death, his estate would pass into SAFE Trusts for his two children. At their deaths, the assets would pass into Dynasty SAFE Trusts for their children. Long after William's demise, his family will be able to appreciate the gift of his generosity and forethought.

An alternative (and simpler) approach to extending SAFE benefits for future generations would be to create one large Dynasty SAFE Trust for the children and their descendants. This Dynasty SAFE Trust would serve as one big pot for the blood and other designated heirs, without the need to distribute to separate Dynasty SAFE Trusts. This option is simpler to

WILLIAM'S REVOCABLE LIVING TRUST WITH SAFE TRUSTS FOR HIS CHILDREN AND DYNASTY TRUSTS AFTER THAT

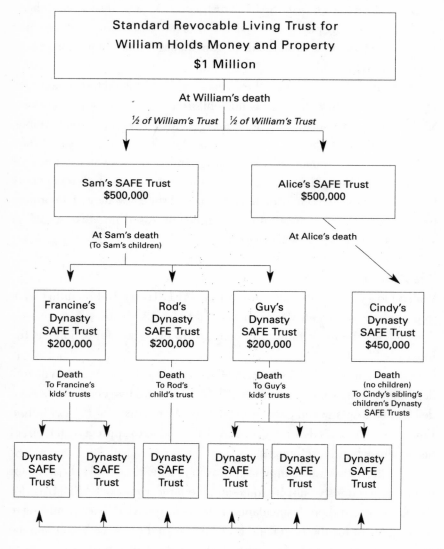

ALTERNATIVE FOR WILLIAM'S CASE, USING ONE DYNASTY SAFE TRUST FOR SAM AND HIS DESCENDANTS, AND ONE DYNASTY SAFE TRUST FOR ALICE AND HER DESCENDANTS

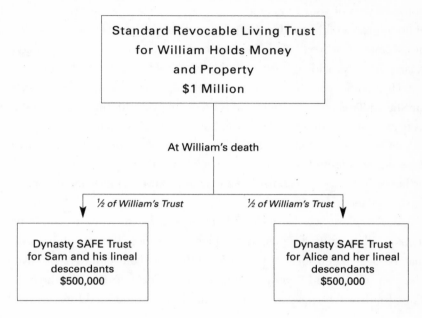

create and administer but does not allow as much flexibility and individualized treatment of different family members.

A SAFE Trust can be used by anyone, regardless of the size of the estate or the amount of assets. But a Dynasty SAFE Trust usually works best with very large estates because of the costs involved in creating Dynasty SAFE Trusts, and the added work involved in administering them. As you can see from the charts on pages 52 and 53, Dynasty SAFE Trusts mean creating more trusts. Depending on your situation, this can add several thousand dollars to your costs above the cost for the regular SAFE Trusts. You typically wouldn't bother with Dynasty SAFE Trusts unless you are leaving at least $100,000 to each of your children.

SAFE Benefit 6: Protection for Nonfamily Members

We've listed key benefits of SAFE Trusts: protections for your *children* (or other descendants) in case they are divorced, die, are sued, or desire privacy.

But what if you don't have children, or you wish to protect others who are not members of your bloodline? For example, perhaps there's an adopted child or grandchild, or a dear friend, for whom you want to provide a SAFE inheritance. Can you? Yes! You *can* create a SAFE Trust for nonblood-related heirs, providing them with the same kinds of valuable benefits.

Here's how you can use it: You would again usually begin with a regular Starter Trust, which you would fund during your lifetime. You can serve as trustee and maintain full control. So far, nothing's changed.

At your death, your estate (or any portion of it) may pass into a SAFE Trust for an adopted relative, or even a friend. This person can serve as his or her own trustee, in control of the assets. And this individual may take money as needed.

If your designated nonblood heir later is divorced, he or she is protected. When your designated nonblood heir dies, the remaining assets may be designated for that person's children, or your children, or anyone else you select. And if your designated nonblood heir is sued, the SAFE Trust funds will be insulated from his/her lawsuits and creditors.

With a SAFE Trust, you are not limited to blood relatives. You can provide the very same SAFE benefits to any person you choose: adopted heirs, friends, and anyone else. The following example illustrates how a SAFE Trust can extend benefits to "extended family."

The Story of Rachel

Rachel and her late husband James had adopted a son, Mark. Rachel wanted to leave her estate to Mark. She wanted to protect Mark's inheritance for Mark in case he was divorced or was sued. And she wished to ensure that Mark's kids inherited at Mark's death, rather than seeing the remainder of her estate pass to Mark's wife.

RACHEL'S REVOCABLE LIVING TRUST
COMBINED WITH A SAFE TRUST

Begins with a Standard Revocable Living Trust for Rachel

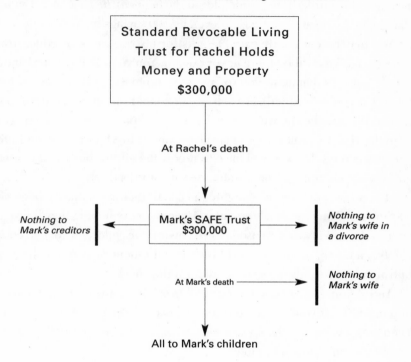

Even though Mark was adopted, Rachel could still provide him with the full range of SAFE protections.

A SAFE Trust can provide the same protections for heirs who are not your blood relatives. It's wonderful to have the assurance that your life savings will be going to and staying with those special individuals in your circle.

In this book, we will typically refer to the benefits of SAFE planning for children and grandchildren, so we do not have to constantly refer to others as well. Please keep in mind, though, SAFE planning can be used to protect anyone you choose.

SAFE Benefit 7: Protections for Kids During Your Life

So far, we've been talking about providing protections for the inheritance you wish to leave for your heirs *when you die*. But perhaps you'd like to make gifts to your kids or grandchildren *during your lifetime*. No, I'm not talking about a tie at Christmas, or even a $100 savings bond.

You may be considering *sizable* gifts for tax reasons—to reduce your estate so that less will be there at your death. You've probably heard about the gift tax rules that allow you to give away up to $12,000 per year (up to $24,000 if you're married) to each of your children, grandchildren, and anyone else you choose, with no tax having to be paid on it, and no reporting to the IRS. In addition, you may give away up to $1 million in your lifetime, with no tax, but you will have to report the gift to the IRS and it will reduce your exemption from estate taxes at your death.

If you give your son or daughter $12,000, that immediately becomes their money. They can freely spend it. Even if you're hoping they'll save it, put it aside, and invest it to use later to cover their children's college costs, or to buy a home, or even to start off their retirement savings, you have no control over the funds once you've written the check.

And if you give money to your children, there are no protections to keep it SAFE. If your child later gets a divorce, the spouse may get half. When your child dies, the spouse may get it all. And if your child is sued, your gifted funds are vulnerable.

Is there any way to make gifts to kids but still keep control? And can you provide bloodline protections at the same time? The ideal answer could be a Crummey SAFE Trust.

The name Crummey was chosen not because it describes the poor quality of this trust but because D. Clifford Crummey was involved in the case (*Crummey v. Commissioner*, 9th Cir. 1968) that established that these types of trusts work.

Up until now, the SAFE Trusts that we've discussed have all been combined with Starter Trusts. You would establish a Revocable Living Trust (or some other Starter Trust), which you control during your life; at death, your trust assets distribute to SAFE Trusts for the kids. But a Crummey SAFE Trust is different.

You can establish a Crummey SAFE Trust for the benefit of a child or grandchild, *if* you meet certain requirements. First, the trust must be irrevocable, unchangeable. You can't change your mind once it's done. Second, you create it now and put assets (make gifts) into it now, while you are alive. Third, you can't be the trustee if you are making the gifts. But you *can* be the trustee if your spouse is the one making the gifts into the trust. In fact, your spouse can gift $12,000 for herself *and* $12,000 on your behalf (using your $12,000 tax-free allotment) into a Crummey SAFE Trust, with you serving as the trustee.

As the trustee, you're in control. You can determine the investments, and you can decide if and when to release any of the funds to your child (or grandchild). You maintain control, but the assets are no longer in your estate. If you have to go to a nursing home, the assets are not considered yours. At your death, the assets are not taxable.

And since the funds are in a Crummey SAFE Trust, they get all the usual SAFE protections. If your child gets a divorce, or dies, or is sued, the funds are insulated. The story of Martin and Sylvia shows how a Crummey SAFE Trust works.

The Story of Martin and Sylvia

Martin and Sylvia had a nice estate. Not huge, but more than they'd need during their lifetimes. The income from their private and government pensions was more than enough to satisfy their costs.

They were interested in giving away as much as possible to their children and grandchildren. But if they just gave money away outright, their children's or grandchildren's spouses, or others outside the family, could wind up with their money. That's not what Martin and Sylvia wanted. And they certainly didn't want to give any significant amounts to their immature teenage grandkids. Crummey SAFE Trusts provided the perfect solution.

They had two children and three grandchildren, and they could give up to $24,000 to each—$120,000 in total per year. They created five Crummey SAFE Trusts, one for each child and grandchild, and named Sylvia as the trustee. Martin made the gifts.

Over the years, Martin periodically made gifts to the Crummey SAFE

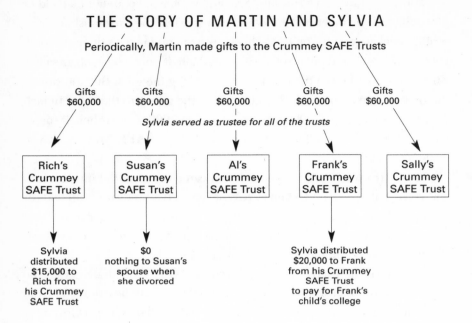

THE STORY OF MARTIN AND SYLVIA

Periodically, Martin made gifts to the Crummey SAFE Trusts

| Gifts $60,000 | Gifts $60,000 | Gifts $60,000 | Gifts $60,000 | Gifts $60,000 |

Sylvia served as trustee for all of the trusts

| Rich's Crummey SAFE Trust | Susan's Crummey SAFE Trust | Al's Crummey SAFE Trust | Frank's Crummey SAFE Trust | Sally's Crummey SAFE Trust |

| Sylvia distributed $15,000 to Rich from his Crummey SAFE Trust | $0 nothing to Susan's spouse when she divorced | | Sylvia distributed $20,000 to Frank from his Crummey SAFE Trust to pay for Frank's child's college | |

Trusts. Not every year, and not always $24,000. The trust funds were invested and grew.

When a child needed money, Sylvia could make a distribution from that child's Crummey SAFE Trust. She used the money to help one child buy a car, and a grandchild to pay for college. When one child divorced, the Crummey SAFE Trust was protected and could not be included in the split of the joint marital assets.

At Sylvia's death, each child and adult grandchild would become trustee of his or her own Crummey SAFE Trusts. At each child's or grandchild's death, if anything was left, it would pass out of the trust to the child's or grandchild's children.

For many people, Crummey SAFE Trusts are the best, most protective way to make family gifts. Too often, parents have lamented to me how the gifts made to their children have been squandered, or lost in a divorce, or left to the child's spouse (whom the parents didn't particularly like) at death. By using a Crummey SAFE Trust, you can make gifts to benefit your children or grandchildren, reducing the size of your estate that can be taxed at your death, while gaining the peace of mind of knowing that you have avoided dangerous situations for your own family.

We've been discussing fairly standard "vanilla" SAFE planning to protect your family's inheritance from divorce, death, lawsuits, and prying eyes. But there are actually a number of different options that can provide tasty benefits in addition to protection from a child's spouse and creditors. In the next chapters, we'll discuss the most common of these specialized SAFE plans.

PART II

Choosing
the SAFE Plan
to Fit Your
Priorities

CHAPTER 4

Slash Death
and Income Taxes

When you die, Uncle Sam will have his hand out to grab part of your assets before your heirs can enjoy their inheritance. When your children pass on, Uncle Sam's there *again*. When your grandchildren die, you guessed it—Uncle Sam's reaching into *their* pockets. Your assets could be taxed *again,* and *again,* and *again*.

And there are multiple *types* of taxes. At your death, your estate may have to pay federal death taxes, state death taxes, and both federal and state income taxes.

A SAFE plan can keep your money safe from taxes and protected for your family. By taking the right steps, you can reduce or eliminate federal and state death and income taxes. And at the same time, you can turn even a modest IRA, 401(k), or other retirement plan into a multimillion-dollar benefit for your children and grandchildren, through the power of income tax deferral.

How do you get these tax benefits? By using SAFE Trusts, typically in combination with Revocable Living Trusts or other specialized Starter Trusts.

SAFE Tax Saver 1: Death Tax Protection SAFE Trust

No matter how overtaxed or poor you think you are during life, Uncle Sam will want to review your estate at death to make sure you don't owe him that one final tax—the federal estate or death tax. Whether there will be any tax to pay depends on the size of your estate and how your estate plan works. The good news is that most people don't pay this tax at all because the exemption from federal death taxes is $2 million (in 2006). This means the first $2 million left to your heirs is tax-free.

In the typical case, folks leave their estates to their kids outright. The kids get the inheritance, and it becomes theirs. They may spend it, or they may grow it.

When your children die, *their* entire estates are subject to the federal death tax too, including any money that they received as an inheritance. Yes, *you* may die only once, but your money is subject to the death tax *twice*—once at your death and again when your children die. (They say cats have nine lives; it's a good thing *they* don't pay taxes!)

Let's say you leave one of your children $200,000. That's a wonderful gift. But without proper planning at your death, your child might end up with a lot less. If your estate must pay federal death taxes, he only gets about $108,000 (assuming a 46 percent estate tax)—Uncle Sam takes about $92,000!

But wait, it gets worse. When your child dies, that same $108,000 (if not spent) is subject to *your child's* death taxes. After paying close to $50,000, his heirs wind up with $58,000. Just think about that—your grandchildren wind up with only $58,000 out of the $200,000 you hoped they would receive. No matter what kind of math you use, old or new, that's a lot of subtraction.

Ready for some good news? There is a way to stop the multiplier effect of death taxes; it's a specific SAFE Trust called a Death Tax Protection SAFE Trust. With this unique tool, you can eliminate the double taxation of your life savings. Here's how it works:

Let's take the same example. Say your child receives an inheritance of $108,000 at your death, after the death tax on your estate (don't worry, further on in this chapter we'll tell you how you may reduce or eliminate *your* death tax). Instead of leaving the money to her directly, you leave it in a Death Tax Protection SAFE Trust. Your child gets all the benefits we've already discussed: protections from the spouse in a divorce, protections for the grandkids at your child's death, and protections against lawsuits and creditors. Now let's add one more. With a Death Tax Protection SAFE Trust, your kids can pass on the remains of your estate to their children (your grandchildren) with *no* estate tax. Not only does a Death Tax Protection SAFE Trust protect from ex-spouses and creditors, but it also keeps Uncle Sam's hands out of your kids' pockets.

Ready for even better news?

It's not only the amount of the inheritance you leave that's protected from death taxes when your kids die; it's the *entire growth* on the Death Tax Protection SAFE Trust's investments, regardless of how much.

Continuing with our prior example: Your daughter gets an inheritance of $108,000 in a Death Tax Protection SAFE Trust. She carefully manages it, making prudent investments. She doesn't spend these funds, but instead uses her own money for her expenses. The SAFE Trust money just grows.

At your daughter's death, her Death Tax Protection SAFE Trust has risen to $500,000. At her death, the entire $500,000 passes to her children *free of death taxes*. That's more than $200,000 tax savings!

The Death Tax Protection SAFE Trust is also often called a GST SAFE Trust, with GST standing for Generation Skipping Transfer tax. Don't let the name throw you. With this trust, you're not really skipping a generation with respect to the inheritance: You're still able to leave the inheritance for your kids to enjoy. You're only skipping the death tax at your kids' passing, and that's a great benefit.

In Chapter 3, we explained how a Dynasty SAFE Trust can be used to extend the special family protections beyond your children and grandchildren. You may protect the inheritance from spouses, lawsuits, and creditors for generations to come. *And* by combining a Death Tax Protection SAFE Trust with a Dynasty SAFE Trust, you can protect the inheritance from *taxes* for future generations too.

What's the hitch? Well, it's really not a hitch, but there is a limit. You can only protect up to $2 million in this manner (if you're married, you can each pass $2 million to your kids free of their death taxes). This is a total of $2 million, not $2 million per child. So if you have three kids, you can protect $666,666 for each from being double-taxed using a Death Tax Protection SAFE Trust.

But here's a little-known gem: you don't have to allocate the $2 million tax benefit equally to your kids. Let's say you have two children—one's a doctor, and one's a school teacher. The doctor already has a taxable estate of her own of more than $2 million, but your son the teacher will never get close. He won't need to shelter money from his death taxes, because his smaller estate will never exceed the $2 million exemption, even with the inheritance. In this case, you can designate all of the death tax benefit to the child who needs the protection. You would set up a Death Tax Protection SAFE Trust just for your doctor daughter.

No, you are not being unfair; this uneven allocation of the tax benefit doesn't affect how much money you actually leave to your kids. In this example, you could leave your son and daughter the same amount of money. But your daughter's inheritance would go into the Death Tax Protection SAFE Trust to help protect her estate from a double tax, and your son's would go into a standard SAFE Trust (since his estate won't be taxed anyhow). Let's take another example to illustrate how the Death Tax Protection SAFE Trust works to reduce future taxes on your children's estates.

The Case of Barbara

Barbara and her late husband had accumulated a very nice estate. Barbara lived modestly, but didn't deprive herself. One of her wishes was to leave as much as possible for her three children, Jim, John, and Alice.

Jim and John were doing very well financially. Jim started his own computer consulting business, and had amassed an estate of several million dollars. John was a lawyer, and he was making a very decent income. But Alice worked as a school nurse. She loved her job but was living month to month.

At Barbara's death, she left an estate of about $3 million, split equally among her three children. Because of the size of her estate, $2 million was tax-free, and the remaining $1 million was taxed. At the federal estate tax rate of about 45 percent (in 2007), $450,000 was paid to Uncle Sam, and each child received about $850,000. Not bad!

Barbara was wise, and she created SAFE Trusts for each of them. She very much desired the protections these trusts provided in case her children ever divorced, or at her children's deaths, or in the event of a lawsuit.

She also didn't want her money taxed twice, at her death and again at her children's deaths. Barbara recognized that even with her inheritance, Alice's estate would never reach the $2 million that triggers a death tax (even after receiving her inheritance of $850,000). But Jim and John already had substantial savings, and their inheritances would probably put them over the top.

So Barbara wisely established Death Tax Protection SAFE Trusts for her sons and a standard SAFE Trust for Alice. Here's how the money split up at her death:

BARBARA'S REVOCABLE LIVING TRUST WITH A STANDARD SAFE TRUST FOR ALICE AND DEATH TAX PROTECTION SAFE TRUSTS FOR JIM AND JOHN

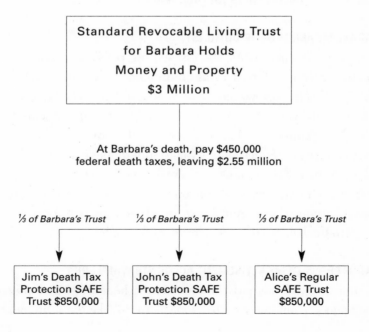

Standard Revocable Living Trust
for Barbara Holds
Money and Property
$3 Million

At Barbara's death, pay $450,000
federal death taxes, leaving $2.55 million

⅓ of Barbara's Trust   ⅓ of Barbara's Trust   ⅓ of Barbara's Trust

| Jim's Death Tax Protection SAFE Trust $850,000 | John's Death Tax Protection SAFE Trust $850,000 | Alice's Regular SAFE Trust $850,000 |

As you can see, each of Barbara's three children received equal portions of the estate. But Jim and John each received their inheritance in a Death Tax Protection SAFE Trust. This is because Barbara was limited to a maximum of $2 million for the death tax protections.

When Barbara's children died, Jim and John were each able to pass the entire amount in their Death Tax Protection SAFE Trusts to their children free of tax. And Alice's passed free of tax because her estate value was under the death tax exemption amount at that time. Through careful planning, Barbara was able to maximize the value of her children's inheritance. You can, and *should,* do no less.

SAFE Tax Saver 2: Retirement Fund SAFE Trust

How would you like to turn your modest IRA, 401(k), 403(b), pension, or profit-sharing plan into a multimillion-dollar benefit for your children or grandchildren? You can, and it's even legal! Believe it or not, federal law, good planning, and a Retirement Fund SAFE Trust make it possible for most Americans, even retirees living on modest retirement accounts, to multiply their IRAs, 401(k)s, 403(b)s, and other retirement plans by as much as ten or twenty times for their heirs.

WHAT ARE MINIMUM DISTRIBUTIONS?

The primary benefit of IRAs, 401(k)s, 403(b)s, pensions, and profit-sharing plans (collectively referred to as "retirement funds" or "retirement accounts") is that they grow *income tax–deferred.* You do pay income tax, but only at the time you withdraw funds. Until then, the investments grow tax-free in your account, speeding its growth. So that you don't get too much of a good thing, Uncle Sam requires you to start dipping into your retirement funds by April 1 of the year after you reach age 70½. The amount you must withdraw each year for the rest of your life is calculated by dividing a complicated version of your remaining life expectancy (set forth on an IRS table) into the balance of your retirement accounts.

WHAT HAPPENS TO MY RETIREMENT ACCOUNTS WHEN I DIE?

Your retirement funds pass to your named beneficiaries at your death. Without good planning, your heirs may have to take the retirement funds out within a short time after your death, because of tax law requirements, creating a hefty income tax bill (calculated at your child's tax rate) and losing any future tax-deferred growth.

But by setting up your IRAs and other retirement accounts properly, and naming the right beneficiaries, you should be able to allow your beneficiaries to stretch out withdrawals over their lifetimes, while getting the SAFE Trust protections we discussed earlier. This is often called a Super or Stretch IRA SAFE Trust, or a Retirement Fund SAFE Trust. Note that some retirement plans, like 401(k)s and 403(b)s, may not allow the same flexibility for stretching out withdrawals, so check with the plan administrators. You may have to roll these into IRAs if you want your beneficiaries to be able to stretch withdrawals.

Let's see how this benefit can work for you. Say you have $125,000 in your IRA at the time you pass away. Your grandchild, age ten, is named as the beneficiary. Beginning the year following your death, the law requires him (or more accurately, a guardian for him) to start taking at least minimum distributions based on your grandchild's life expectancy (though he can take more if needed).

At age eleven (a year after your death), your grandchild has a 71.8-year life expectancy. This means your grandchild would only have to take 1/71.8 of the total the first year, 1/70.8 the second year, 1/69.8 the third year, and so on. Assuming the IRA is yielding 7 percent annually, the account will grow phenomenally over the years.

If your grandchild takes only the minimum distributions each year, by age sixty-five the IRA account would have grown to more than $1,300,000. And the minimum distributions taken by your grandchild (if those distributions earn 5 percent after tax) would total about $1,700,000. In other words, you've been able to turn your $125,000 IRA into a $3 million benefit for your heir!

You may name children instead of grandchildren as beneficiaries. But since their life expectancies won't be as long, their minimum distributions will have to be higher. And that means the growth of your retirement accounts won't be as dramatic.

There's no age limit on when you can add or change the name of a beneficiary. Even if you're already seventy-five, eighty, or older, and well into the time when you have begun to take minimum distributions for yourself, you can still engage in this planning to benefit children or grandchildren.

WHEN DOES THE RETIREMENT FUND SAFE TRUST COME IN?

Yes, without using a SAFE Trust you can still obtain the benefit of the extended payout for the lifetimes of children and grandchildren just by naming them as beneficiaries on your retirement accounts. But you can really supercharge the growth of your dollars and better protect your heirs by creating a Retirement Fund SAFE Trust for the kids or grandkids and naming this trust as beneficiary of your retirement accounts instead.

Benefit 1: Management for Youngsters

A Retirement Fund SAFE Trust allows you to provide management for young kids or grandkids until they're old enough to manage for themselves. Without a SAFE Trust, they get control at the age of majority (typically eighteen) and can spend the entire retirement account at once. At eighteen, it's a lot of fun to take the money and travel with friends, buy an expensive sports car, and party, party, party. When the youngsters are older, they may look back and wish they had taken only the required minimum distributions, letting the rest of the money grow to awesome amounts. But once the retirement funds have been frittered away, it's too late.

With a Retirement Fund SAFE Trust, you can pick a trustee (perhaps a grandchild's parent—your child) to manage the funds and determine the distributions until the grandchild is mature enough to handle the money himself: maybe age twenty-five, or thirty . . . or sixty! The Retirement Fund SAFE Trust makes it more likely that the funds will not be squandered long before a youngster is wise enough to appreciate their value.

Benefit 2: Standard SAFE Trust Protections

If you name the children or grandchildren as direct beneficiaries on your retirement accounts without creating a Retirement Fund SAFE Trust, they will miss out on the important SAFE protections that "bulletproof" the inheritance against attacks by spouses, creditors, and lawsuits. But naming the

Retirement Fund SAFE Trust as beneficiary of your retirement accounts gains for your family all the protections discussed in Chapter 3.

Benefit 3: Avoid Unnecessary Probate

A Retirement Fund SAFE Trust enables your heirs to avoid an unnecessary probate. If you simply name your child as beneficiary, the IRA or other retirement account might have to be probated when your child dies. Many retirement plans and IRAs do not allow the beneficiaries to name subsequent beneficiaries. With a Retirement Fund SAFE Trust as beneficiary, no probate will be required at your children's deaths.

Molly's case nicely illustrates how the Retirement Fund SAFE Trust can work wonders for your family, even with a rather modest retirement account.

The Case of Molly

Molly was sixty-four when she set up her Retirement Fund SAFE Trust. She created the trust by executing the document with her estate-planning lawyer but did not put the IRA into the trust. Instead, she contacted the bank where the IRA was held and changed the name of the beneficiary to be her Retirement Fund SAFE Trust.

At sixty-four, her IRA had $65,000, which was made up of two bank CDs. She didn't touch her IRA until she reached age 70½, at which time she started taking her minimum distributions, as required by law. At that time, her IRA had grown to $78,000.

Molly's entire estate was about $400,000. She wanted most of her assets to go to her son Nathan. So she established a regular SAFE Trust for her other (nonretirement fund) assets. But she desired to leave something directly to her granddaughter, Lindsay, and the IRA was the best asset, because the Retirement Fund SAFE Trust would allow Lindsay unparalleled income tax benefits, using her long life expectancy.

At the time Molly created the Retirement Fund SAFE Trust, Lindsay was just ten years old. She was a wonderful child, but too young to responsibly manage the inheritance on her own. So Molly set up the Retirement Fund SAFE Trust naming Lindsay's father, Nathan, as trustee. Molly's trust instructed that only the minimum required distributions (based on Lindsay's life expectancy at the time of Molly's death) be taken from the IRA funds, unless Lindsay needed (truly needed) more. She gave the trustee the option to take more than the minimum distributions but hoped that would not be necessary.

Molly died at age seventy-five, and at that time her IRA was down to $60,000. Lindsay was twenty-one and just finishing college. If she had been trustee of her Retirement Fund SAFE Trust, she might have been tempted to grab the entire $60,000 and take an extended vacation. But Nathan had control, and he gave her only what she needed to supplement the income she was earning at the advertising agency she had joined.

Nathan wisely managed the Retirement Fund SAFE Trust for nine years, until Lindsay's thirtieth birthday. Molly had set up the trust so that at that time Lindsay could take over as her own trustee. Molly had made an educated guess, figuring that by thirty Lindsay would be mature enough to handle the funds herself, and she was right.

Lindsay married, had two kids, and the family managed pretty well. Over the years, Lindsay and her husband supplemented their income as necessary from the Retirement Fund SAFE Trust. When Lindsay reached age sixty-four, she and her husband retired. Molly's foresight had assured them a pleasant retirement. At that time, Molly's IRA and the Retirement Fund SAFE Trust had about $335,000 (assuming a 7 percent return). The money had grown through prudent investments and the tax-deferred magic of the Retirement Fund SAFE Trust. In addition, Lindsay had received distributions of $341,000 over the years (with a 5 percent after-tax return).

So Molly's little $60,000 IRA at her death had created a wonderful inheritance of more than $675,000 for her granddaughter. What a loving gift!

Note: You cannot put your IRAs and other retirement accounts directly into a trust while you're alive. Only *you* can own your IRA and receive the income tax deferral. But a trust *can* be named as the beneficiary.

If you are married, typically you'd name your spouse as the primary beneficiary of your retirement accounts, and the Retirement Fund SAFE Trust as secondary. If you die before your spouse, she can roll your IRA into her own IRA, continue the income tax deferral, then leave it to the Retirement Fund SAFE Trust when she dies. If your spouse predeceases

MOLLY'S CASE

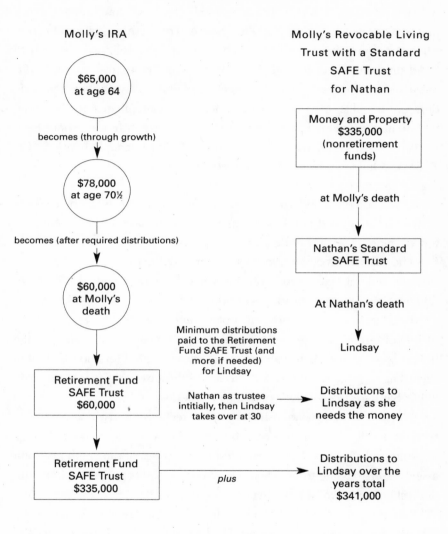

Molly's IRA

$65,000 at age 64

becomes (through growth)

$78,000 at age 70½

becomes (after required distributions)

$60,000 at Molly's death

Retirement Fund SAFE Trust $60,000

Retirement Fund SAFE Trust $335,000

Molly's Revocable Living Trust with a Standard SAFE Trust for Nathan

Money and Property $335,000 (nonretirement funds)

at Molly's death

Nathan's Standard SAFE Trust

At Nathan's death

Lindsay

Minimum distributions paid to the Retirement Fund SAFE Trust (and more if needed) for Lindsay

Nathan as trustee intitially, then Lindsay takes over at 30

Distributions to Lindsay as she needs the money

plus

Distributions to Lindsay over the years total $341,000

you, then at your death your IRA would pay to the secondary beneficiary, the Retirement Fund SAFE Trust.

And if you're not married, just name the Retirement Fund SAFE Trust as primary beneficiary on your retirement accounts. It's a win for you and a big win for your kids and grandkids!

SAFE Tax Saver 3: A-B Trust and SAFE Trust

As we've discussed, SAFE Trusts generally are not "stand-alone" documents. They usually are attached to a Starter Trust, created by and for you. The most common is the old Revocable Living Trust designed primarily to avoid probate. We discussed Revocable Living Trusts in Chapter 1. But there are many different types of specialized Starter Trusts, which provide different benefits for you and your spouse. You can enhance the planning for you and your family by combining SAFE Trusts with other specialized Starter Trusts. Here, we'll tell you how A-B Trusts coupled with SAFE Trusts can help you reduce or eliminate *your* death tax exposure, preserving the maximum for your family.

When you die, children, lawyers, and probate courts won't be the only ones with their hands out. Uncle Sam may take the largest share—through the infamous estate tax or death tax.

The costs of processing your estate through the probate court pale beside the federal taxes your estate may have to pay at your death. Rates range from 45 percent to 46 percent (in 2006).

Don't get confused between probate and death taxes. They're completely different. Probate is the process of passing assets at death through the probate court to assure all the assets are accounted for and distributed according to your wishes. Death taxes are the taxes you pay at death to Uncle Sam, for the privilege of dying in America.

You may avoid probate using any of the techniques discussed in Chapter 1 and still owe a huge death tax. Whether your assets pass through or avoid probate, they still are counted for purposes of the death tax. Joint assets, assets passing to beneficiaries, and even assets passing to heirs under a standard Revocable Living Trust—all are subject to death taxes.

Not everyone has to worry about federal death taxes. Right now, each taxpayer gets a death tax exemption, which means your estate will pay federal death taxes only if it exceeds $2 million in 2006. And the credit rises to $3.5 million in 2009. In 2010, the federal death tax is entirely eliminated. And then in 2011, the death tax comes back, with an exemption of $1 million.

That's if Congress doesn't change the rules again.

If your estate is under $1 million, chances are you won't have to worry about the death tax, no matter when you die. But don't turn the page yet. When you add things up, you may be surprised at just how large your estate really is.

For example, in many parts of the country the market value of even a modest home can exceed $600,000—and it doesn't take much more in the way of other assets to bump you up over that $1 million mark.

Many people forget to figure the proceeds that will be paid from life insurance policies when totaling up the value of their estates. If you have total assets (house, car, stocks, cash, etc.) of $800,000, plus another few hundred thousand in life insurance, your estate could end up paying a hefty chunk in federal death taxes.

And don't forget lump-sum pension benefits or money you may inherit. If your estate currently totals $600,000 but a parent or other relative dies and leaves you a substantial asset—a house, for example—you may suddenly find yourself in the federal death tax category.

If you're married and you leave everything to each other, as most people do, there's no federal death tax at the first death, no matter how large the estate (though special rules apply to surviving noncitizen spouses). You could leave a billion dollars to your spouse with no death tax. But leaving everything outright to the spouse can be a costly mistake, as happened to Douglas and Jeri.

The Story of Douglas and Jeri

Douglas and Jeri had a total estate of $2.5 million. When Doug died, he left everything to his wife, Jeri. There was no death tax at that time, because there's no estate tax on assets left to a spouse. But he had created a future problem. Jeri had the entire $2.5 million. At her death in 2006, she left everything to her children. By law, her estate was able to automatically exempt $2 million from the federal death tax, but the remaining $500,000 was subject to tax. As a result, her estate paid federal death taxes of about $230,000.

We're not talking pennies here. That tax amount is huge. And to think that the tax payment was totally *unnecessary*. With an A-B Starter Trust (at a cost of perhaps $2,500 to $3,500), combined with a SAFE Trust, the entire $230,000 death tax could have been avoided, protecting the full amount of your estate for your family.

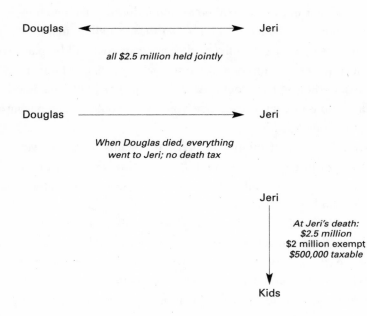

DOUGLAS AND JERI
NO TRUST

Douglas ◄─────────────────► Jeri

all $2.5 million held jointly

Douglas ─────────────────► Jeri

When Douglas died, everything
went to Jeri; no death tax

Jeri

│
│ *At Jeri's death:*
│ *$2.5 million*
│ *$2 million exempt*
│ *$500,000 taxable*
▼

Kids

**At Jeri's death, she left $2.5 million to the kids. Since it was more
than the $2 million exemption (in 2006), the estate paid
a huge tax (about $230,000) on the $500,000.**

In the example of Douglas and Jeri, they used Jeri's $2 million exemption.
But by not planning, they lost Doug's! With an A-B Trust, you can use *both*
your and your spouse's federal death tax exemptions. If the death tax exemption is $2 million, the A-B Trust lets you double-dip—you can get an extra
scoop of tax-exempt assets, bringing you to a total of $4 million. Here's how:

You and your spouse could start by *each* creating your own A-B Starter
Trust. (In some states, a specialized joint A-B Starter Trust may be used.)
Each works much like the standard Revocable Living Trust. You'd typically
be trustee of your trust, your spouse for his (though in some cases, where
one spouse is the money manager for the family, that spouse could be
trustee for both trusts).

Most important, you and your spouse would split your nonretirement fund assets—everything except your IRAs, 401(k)s, 403(b)s, and other retirement accounts—between your two trusts. About half would go into your A-B Trust, half into your spouse's trust.

Let's say you die first. At that time, your A-B Trust would split into an A and a B Trust. Up to the exemption amount ($2 million) would go into your B Trust, and anything over would go into your A Trust. The A Trust usually gets no special tax protection—it just holds the amount in excess of the portion that is exempt from federal death taxes; it basically belongs to your spouse. In fact, you may allow your spouse to pull the entire amount out of your A Trust and put it into her own A-B Trust.

But your B Trust provides the tax benefit. The B Trust becomes irrevocable at your death. Don't let that scare you, though. Your spouse has full control of your B Trust. While your spouse is alive, he can be the trustee (manager) of your B Trust. He gets all the income generated from the investments—interest, dividends, rents, and so forth. And he can take principal as he needs it (for food, clothing, health care, shelter, etc.), or as the kids need it.

When he also dies, the assets in both his A-B Trust and in your A-B Trust automatically go into the SAFE Trusts for the children. But here's the benefit: everything in *your* B Trust passes death tax–free. Plus your spouse can exempt $2 million from federal death taxes. Let's take a look at the story of Dan and Amy to see how this all works.

The Story of Dan and Amy

Dan and Amy each created an A-B Starter Trust. They put $1.5 million into Dan's A-B Trust and $1.5 million into Amy's A-B Trust. That created no problem, because Dan and Amy remained in complete control. At Dan's death, the entire $1.5 million went into his B Trust, and there was nothing to go into his A Trust. Amy remained in control as trustee of Dan's B Trust, as well as her own A-B trust. When Amy died, the money in Dan's B Trust and in Amy's A-B Trust passed into the SAFE Trusts for their kids.

Oh, and what about the death taxes? There were none. That's because the money in Dan's B Trust passed free of any death taxes, using his $2 million exemption from death taxes. And since Amy's assets totaled less than $2 million, there was no tax at all.

DAN'S AND AMY'S A-B TRUSTS
COMBINED WITH SAFE TRUSTS FOR THE CHILDREN

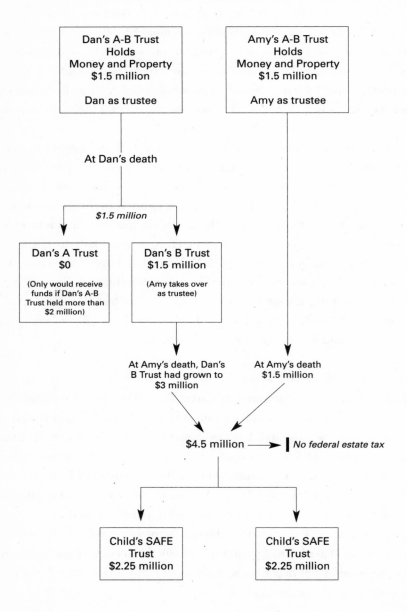

In fact, there was even better news. The $1.5 million in Dan's B Trust had been entirely invested at the time of his death, and it grew to $3 million before Amy died. The entire $3 million in Dan's B Trust, plus the $1.5 million in Amy's A-B Trust, passed free of death taxes. That means they passed $4.5 million to the kids with no tax. Without the A-B Trusts combined with SAFE Trusts, Uncle Sam would have received more than $1.1 million and the kids would not have received the SAFE protections.

What if you and your spouse have more than $4 million? The story of Maria and Hector shows how the A-B Trusts combined with SAFE Trusts would work to protect $4 million, and possibly *more,* from death taxes.

The Story of Maria and Hector

Maria and Hector had done very well, amassing an estate of $5 million. To protect the maximum of $4 million from federal death taxes, they each created A-B Trusts for half the assets.

At Hector's death, his trust split into two trusts: $2 million went into his B Trust (the maximum that could pass free of death taxes), and the remaining $500,000 went into his A Trust. Maria became trustee of both trusts. Over the next several years, she took income from Hector's trusts, and anything more that she needed was taken from her own A-B Trust.

When Maria died, her A-B Trust had grown to $2.8 million, Hector's A Trust was still $500,000, and Hector's B Trust had grown to $2.7 million. Maria's "taxable" estate was $3.3 million (the $2.8 million in her A-B Trust, plus the $500,000 in Hector's A Trust), and the tax was about $600,000 (on the $1.3 million amount over $2 million). The entire $2.7 million in Hector's B Trust, plus $2 million in Maria's A-B Trust, escaped taxation. Their children would end up getting a total of $5.4 million.

SAFE Tax Saver 4: Life Insurance Trust and SAFE Trust

At your death, virtually everything you own is eligible to be included in your taxable estate and then added up to see if it exceeds the death tax exemption amount. This includes your home, CDs, IRAs, 401(k)s, and even life insurance. I've seen folks with fairly modest estates wind up paying many thousands of dollars in death taxes, just because they own life insurance.

Now, don't get me wrong. I'm not knocking life insurance. For many

MARIA'S AND HECTOR'S A-B TRUSTS
COMBINED WITH SAFE TRUSTS FOR THE CHILDREN

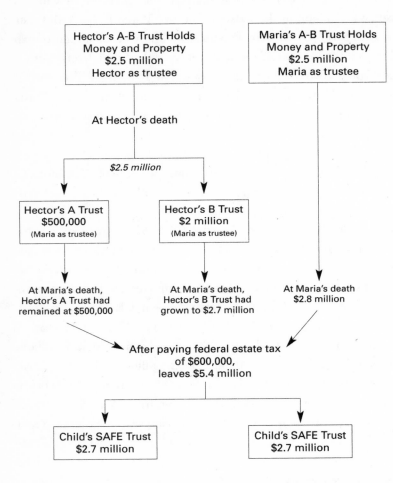

folks, life insurance can be extremely beneficial. But you should be aware that the death benefits are taxable in your estate.

It surprises lots of people to hear this. They've heard that life insurance is not taxable. Don't be confused. Life insurance is not subject to *income taxes*. If you paid premiums of $50,000, and then at your death your heirs receive $250,000, the $200,000 "growth" is not taxable as income. But the entire $250,000 of death benefits are a (tax) horse of a different color and would be considered part of your estate for *death tax* purposes.

If you're wondering whether there's a legal way around this costly scenario, the answer is yes. Although life insurance that you own is taxable at your death, life insurance that is owned by an irrevocable Life Insurance Starter Trust is not taxable. And when you combine a Life Insurance Starter Trust with SAFE Trusts, the proceeds can be paid into SAFE Trusts for your kids *without* any death taxes. Isn't that a better picture? Here's what you'll need to know:

A Life Insurance Trust is very different from most Starter Trusts, including Revocable Living Trusts. Most Starter Trusts are revocable, giving you complete control over and access to all assets in the trust during your life. You can be your own trustee, and you can revoke or change the trust at any time. Not so with a Life Insurance Starter Trust.

With this, you cannot be your own trustee (though your spouse can be the trustee), you cannot have control, and you cannot revoke or change the trust once it's set up. But don't panic, because with the Life Insurance Trust, you don't *need* access to the assets in the trust. While you're alive, all that's in it is a life insurance policy—a piece of paper. There's no money until you die (unless there's some cash value).

How does it work? Let's look at the story of Sam.

Sam's Story

Sam sets up a Life Insurance Trust, which pays into SAFE Trusts for the children when he and his wife Joan both die. The trustee buys a $300,000 policy on his life. His wife Joan is the trustee. Sam contributes $3,500 each year to the trust, which his wife uses to pay the premiums for the insurance policy. (The trustee can be your spouse or other family member, but the tax law may then require the trust to place a few limits on his or her access to the assets; for more flexibility, you may name an unrelated party as trustee.)

If the Life Insurance Trust is properly set up, Sam's contributions to it are free of any gift tax. When Sam dies, the $300,000 insurance benefit will be paid to the Life Insurance Trust. Since Sam is married, income derived from the trust principal, and even the principal itself, can be made available to Joan during her lifetime. On Joan's death, the remaining

SAM'S LIFE INSURANCE TRUST
COMBINED WITH SAFE TRUSTS FOR THE CHILDREN

Joan is trustee

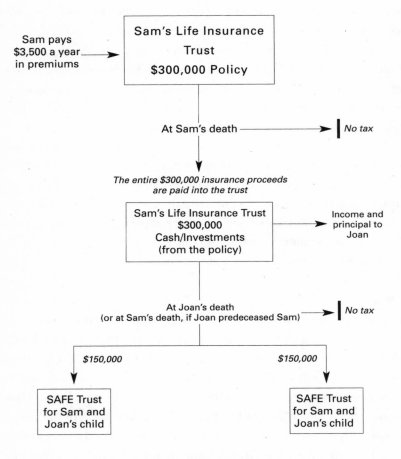

Sam pays $3,500 a year in premiums →

Sam's Life Insurance Trust $300,000 Policy

At Sam's death ————→ | *No tax*

The entire $300,000 insurance proceeds are paid into the trust

Sam's Life Insurance Trust $300,000 Cash/Investments (from the policy)

→ Income and principal to Joan

At Joan's death (or at Sam's death, if Joan predeceased Sam) ——→ | *No tax*

$150,000

$150,000

SAFE Trust for Sam and Joan's child

SAFE Trust for Sam and Joan's child

Bottom Line: The $300,000 of life insurance passes into the children's SAFE Trusts free of any death taxes.

investments will pass into SAFE Trusts for the kids. And the benefit is that the $300,000 can pass to the children's SAFE Trusts without contributing to Sam's and Joan's taxable estates.

NEW POLICY VS. EXISTING POLICY

Note: If Sam placed an existing life insurance policy into the Life Insurance Trust instead of having the trust buy a new policy, there is a "waiting" period: he would have to live at least three years after setting up the trust and transferring ownership of the policy to the trust in order for the proceeds not to be counted in his taxable estate. (There are some complicated techniques to transfer an existing policy into the trust with no waiting period.) If he'd rather not gamble on his life expectancy, he can authorize the trustee of the Life Insurance Trust to buy a new policy, and then no waiting period applies.

SINGLE LIFE POLICY VS. SECOND-TO-DIE POLICY

In the case described above, the life insurance policy in the Life Insurance Trust was on Sam's life. A "single life" insurance policy like Sam's works well, and can save significant death taxes. But you might do even better if you opt for a "second-to-die" insurance policy instead.

The insurance industry is very sharp, and they came up with a product specifically designed just to save your family estate or death taxes and to leave a larger legacy for your children. It's called "second-to-die," or "survivor," insurance.

Unlike insurance on just one person's life, it insures the lives of both spouses. There's no payoff when the first spouse dies. The policy doesn't pay a penny until you have both gone to your higher reward.

Because there's no payoff until *both* you and your spouse die, the insurance company gets to hold on to your money longer. And because the insurance company can hold (and invest) your money longer, you get more insurance for your premium dollar. Let's look at an example.

The Case of Paula and Ron

Paula and Ron are in their early fifties. For a $1 million, one-time premium, they bought a $14 million "second-to-die" life insurance policy.

And of course they had their Life Insurance Trust buy the policy to avoid death taxes.

Now, don't get scared off by the numbers. A big example is dramatic, but you can buy any size policy. In your fifties, a $100,000 lump sum premium would buy you more than $1 million of insurance; a $10,000 premium would get you more than $100,000 of insurance. What's important is the leveraging.

And you don't have to pay the premium in a lump sum. In fact, in most cases it would be advisable *not* to pay one lump sum. Instead, you could pay much smaller and affordable annual premiums. No matter when you die, even if you're still paying premiums, the insurance pays off in full. So if you and your spouse died prematurely, you'd have made a tremendous investment. For example, if you bought a $1 million policy, but paid only $20,000 in premiums before passing on, think of the fabulous return on your money (unfortunately, though, you won't be around to enjoy it).

Let's go back to the case of Paula and Ron. When both of them are gone, that huge pot of money will pay into SAFE Trusts for their kids. In fact, since they were really leveraging up with a large policy, they combined the SAFE Trusts with Dynasty SAFE Trusts. In this way, the insurance proceeds will be available to their children, grandchildren, and great-grandchildren, protected from the spouses and creditors of their blood descendants. If their child, grandchild, or great-grandchild gets divorced or dies, the in-laws can be precluded from getting any of this pot of insurance proceeds.

And they've beaten the federal estate tax system by taking money that would have been taxable to pay premiums for insurance that will not be taxable. They avoid death taxes—not just for themselves but for their heirs for generations!

We'll talk more in Chapter 7 about the benefits of combining several different trusts in one trust document or plan.

Note that for a Life Insurance Trust holding "second-to-die" insurance, a child, some other family member, or a bank may serve as trustee, but it is strictly forbidden for either spouse to serve as the trustee.

When you were young, life insurance provided an excellent tool to make sure your spouse and children were sufficiently cared for in case of your unexpected demise. As you get older, life insurance can be a wise

PAULA AND RON'S LIFE INSURANCE TRUST FOR "SECOND-TO-DIE" INSURANCE COMBINED WITH SAFE TRUSTS AND DYNASTY SAFE TRUSTS FOR CHILDREN AND DESCENDANTS

Rob (their son) serves as trustee

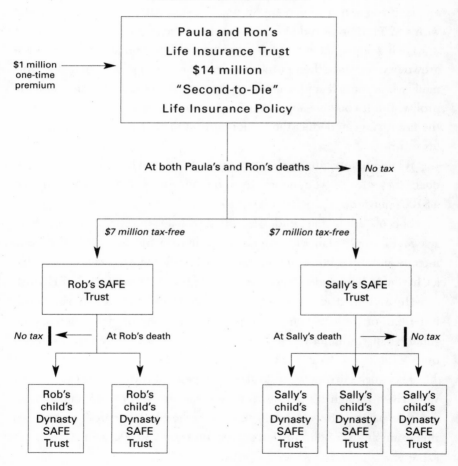

$1 million one-time premium →

Paula and Ron's
Life Insurance Trust
$14 million
"Second-to-Die"
Life Insurance Policy

At both Paula's and Ron's deaths → No tax

$7 million tax-free

$7 million tax-free

Rob's SAFE Trust

Sally's SAFE Trust

No tax ← At Rob's death

At Sally's death → No tax

Rob's child's Dynasty SAFE Trust

Rob's child's Dynasty SAFE Trust

Sally's child's Dynasty SAFE Trust

Sally's child's Dynasty SAFE Trust

Sally's child's Dynasty SAFE Trust

investment to leverage up an inheritance for your heirs. And when combined with a SAFE Trust, or a Dynasty SAFE Trust, you can provide those wonderful SAFE protections for your children and descendants, while reducing or eliminating death taxes too.

SAFE Tax Saver 5: Charitable Trust

Many Americans wish to help charitable organizations. To encourage charitable giving, the government makes your charitable gifts tax-deductible. In other words, Uncle Sam will help pay for part of your contributions. For example, if you're in a 25 percent tax bracket, your $100 gift will be rewarded with a $25 refund or reduction in taxes from the IRS next April.

Giving appreciated property—such as stocks or real estate that have grown in value since their purchase—may carry even greater benefits. Normally when you sell appreciated property, you'll pay capital gains tax on the profits. But if you give appreciated assets to charity, not only can you skip the taxes, you can deduct the higher current market value on your income tax return.

While lifetime gifts to charity provide wonderful benefits to persons in need, they still cost you money. Even though you may get a $25 refund on a $100 contribution, you're still out $75.

Lots of people don't understand that with an appropriate, comprehensive SAFE estate plan, they can benefit a charity while increasing their own income and still protecting their family. This gift-giving power tool is called a Charitable Remainder Trust combined with a Life Insurance SAFE Trust.

Here's how it works: Say you own $200,000 of stock—maybe it was inherited, or perhaps you bought it years ago. The original price, or the value when you inherited it, was $20,000, so you're lucky that it's grown quite a bit.

The stock currently pays a skimpy 1 percent dividend, or $2,000 per year. Even though it's paying so poorly, if you were to sell and reinvest you'd be paying a huge capital gains tax on the $180,000 profit or gain—in this example, $27,000 (15 percent tax on the $180,000 gain). That's not skimpy!

So instead let's plug in this gift-giving power tool: after selecting the lucky charity that will eventually receive your funds, you create a Charitable Remainder Trust and place your $200,000 of stock in the trust. The trust then sells the stock, receives the cash, and pays no tax. While *you* would have had to pay tax on the gain, the trust does not. The cash is now invested conservatively in assets (perhaps an assortment of stocks or mutual funds) generating a 5 percent annual return—$10,000 per year. What have you gained? During your lifetime, you have radically increased your income ($10,000 vs. $2,000). You are entitled to an immediate and sizable charitable deduction, which can reduce your income tax. And at your death, the charity gets the principal in the trust. Now that's a powerful boost.

So far, this plan is a win for charity and a win for you. But your children or other heirs are out up to $200,000. (It's up to $200,000 because if your estate is large enough to pay federal estate tax, your heirs would have received something less than the $200,000 after tax.)

If you also wish to protect your children's inheritance, there's another step you can take. Instead of keeping the entire $10,000 per year of income from the Charitable Remainder Trust, you can buy a $200,000 life insurance policy for, say, $5,000 per year. You buy the policy in a Life Insurance Trust combined with a SAFE Trust to make sure the insurance is not taxed and your family gets the full range of SAFE protections for the proceeds. With this SAFE plan, everyone wins. At your death, your heirs will be happy because they receive $200,000 from the life insurance (not reduced by your death taxes) with SAFE Trust protections; the charity will be happy because it still gets $200,000, and while you are alive you are almost as happy because you now keep the remaining income of $5,000 per year from the Charitable Remainder Trust, a sum still well ahead of the $2,000 you were previously getting from your old stocks.

Of course, not everyone can make charitable giving a win-win-win strategy. This plan works best with appreciated assets generating low income. And to buy life insurance, you must be healthy enough to qualify. But for some people, this is a tax-savings technique that makes a lot of sense (and cents).

CHAPTER 5

Protecting Young or Disabled Beneficiaries

s your child unable to hold on to money? Perhaps your son has a drug or alcohol problem, and any money he gets his hands on goes to the bar or up in smoke. Or maybe your daughter is just a spendthrift. Since shopping is her favorite hobby, thinking responsibly about saving or investing is not likely.

Usually children who can't manage money lack the discipline to plan for the future. As a result, they're never able to get ahead. When you're a caring parent, you're faced with a dilemma: You'd like to help your child out at your death. But if you leave an inheritance outright to a child who can't manage money, chances are the money will disappear quickly. And that future safety net you had intended to establish would be gone.

A child with disabilities or special needs also requires special legal planning. What will happen when you're no longer able to care for the child? Not only will leaving an inheritance to a disabled child create management issues, but the inheritance also may cause the child to lose eligibility for critically needed public benefits.

For a child who can't manage money or who has special needs, SAFE planning is imperative.

MANAGED SAFE TRUSTS

The SAFE Trusts we've discussed so far allow the children to serve as their own trustees, maintaining control over their inheritance. That's the most common way to set up a SAFE Trust. But sometimes that's not the best way to go.

If your child is allowed to serve as his own trustee, and to have free access to the inheritance, he may quickly spend it out of the trust, just as he would if it had been left to him outright. No, a child who can't manage money cannot be allowed to serve as his own trustee. Instead, you should appoint a third-party trustee, creating a Managed SAFE Trust. The third-party trustee may manage the SAFE Trust for your child's whole life, or until your child is old enough to manage for himself.

There's another situation in which a third-party trustee may be needed. If your child is too easily influenced by the spouse, he or she could be convinced to strip the assets out of a standard SAFE Trust, and the benefits you tried to establish would be undone.

You have to ask yourself: Would your child take his entire inheritance out of the SAFE Trust, contrary to your wishes and in violation of the terms of the trust, forfeiting the valuable protections for himself and his children, if pressured by his spouse? Be honest when you answer. If your response is yes, then, again, a third-party trustee for a Managed SAFE Trust is advisable.

In a Managed SAFE Trust, a third-party trustee would handle the investments and make sure the money is making more money. And a third party would distribute the funds to your child under the rules you've set up in the trust.

How do you want the inheritance paid out? You decide. You could provide that your child gets all the income generated by the investments (interest and dividends), but no principal. Or you could give him the income and a fixed amount or percentage of the principal as well. For example, you might give him all of the income, and 3 percent of the principal balance each year.

Depending on the trustee, you might wish to provide the trustee with a degree of discretion. For example, a common approach would be to instruct the trustee to distribute income or principal to your son for his reasonable needs: food, clothing, shelter, health care, and/or education. Or you might combine fixed payments with discretionary distributions, perhaps instructing the trustee to pay all the income to your child, plus any additional principal that the trustee decides, in his discretion, that your child needs. The goal is to make the funds last for a while—you hope, for your child's entire lifetime. Using a Managed SAFE Trust with a third-party trustee may be the perfect solution.

Who should serve as the trustee? This is a very important question. The most common options include:

- One or more of your other children
- Other family members (aunts, uncles, cousins, etc.)
- Friends
- Professionals (your accountant, attorney, or financial adviser)
- Banks and other institutions

Most parents prefer family members. For example, if your son needs an independent trustee for his Managed SAFE Trust, you might select his sister, or a committee of his siblings. The advantage of using siblings is that they care (you hope), they know and love your son (you hope), and they will want to do the right thing (you hope). They may also be willing to serve as trustee without compensation, or at least for an amount of compensation less than a professional or bank would charge.

The primary negative to selecting another family member is that it may put that family member in a very awkward position and create strains that could damage their relationship. It's tough enough for a child to be told that his parents have decided to leave his inheritance in a Managed SAFE Trust with someone else in control, but it's often that much worse when the controlling person is the child's sister or brother.

And you have to consider whether one of your children would really be able to say no to his or her sibling. When you name one child as trustee for another, the word they must be comfortable with is *no*. "No, you can't have more than I'm distributing, because you'll blow it, and there won't be enough money left to take care of you in the future." Not everyone is comfortable saying no to a sibling.

If there's not an appropriate family member, you may name an institutional trustee. Banks and brokers often have huge trust departments. They manage billions of dollars of other folks' money. They should be good at it, because that's what they do. They'll charge the trust for their work, often ½ of 1 percent to 1 percent of the value of the trust assets per year. But they can certainly say no to your child when he asks for money. And if they make a mistake or do something wrong, they have deep pockets. They have sufficient funds to make good on the error. We'll talk more about selecting trustees in Chapter 7.

Regardless of whom you choose as trustee, a Managed SAFE Trust with a third-party trustee is the best way to leave an inheritance for a child who is unable to handle money responsibly himself.

A real case should help illustrate.

The Case of Andy

Larry and Edie's estate totaled about $500,000, including their home, IRAs, and insurance. They planned to enjoy their retirement, and to spend as much as they desired. Anything left would go to their three children: Ken, Eileen, and Andy.

Ken and Eileen were responsible adults, and each could manage his/her inheritance just fine. Andy was another story. He had a drinking problem and found it hard to keep a job for very long. He'd work for a while, then the drinking would get him fired. Larry and Edie were constantly being "hit up" for help.

While Larry and Edie were disappointed in Ken, they still loved him. And he was a good son. He just couldn't keep a job and was always in debt. They didn't want to cut Andy out of the estate, but leaving him an inheritance that would be drunk away in weeks made no sense either.

So they established a Managed SAFE Trust for Andy, to hold his inheritance when they died. Clearly, Andy couldn't serve as trustee. Eileen had the closest relationship to Andy, she understood his problems, and she deeply cared for him. But she could also be firm, and she could stand up to him when necessary. She was the right choice to serve as the trustee for Andy's Managed SAFE Trust.

While Eileen was best, Ken could also handle the job. So he was named as Eileen's alternate, to take over in case Eileen couldn't serve as the trustee for any reason.

LARRY AND EDIE'S REVOCABLE LIVING TRUST WITH REGULAR SAFE TRUSTS FOR TWO CHILDREN AND A MANAGED SAFE TRUST FOR ANDY

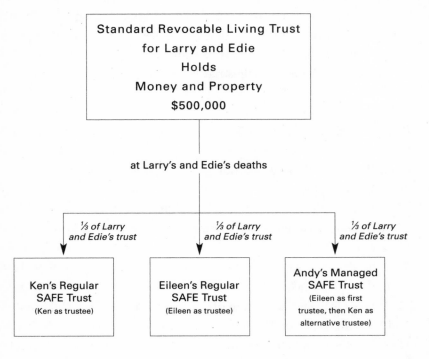

Standard Revocable Living Trust for Larry and Edie
Holds
Money and Property
$500,000

at Larry's and Edie's deaths

⅓ of Larry and Edie's trust

⅓ of Larry and Edie's trust

⅓ of Larry and Edie's trust

Ken's Regular SAFE Trust
(Ken as trustee)

Eileen's Regular SAFE Trust
(Eileen as trustee)

Andy's Managed SAFE Trust
(Eileen as first trustee, then Ken as alternative trustee)

Bottom Line: All three children inherit with standard SAFE protections, and assets are managed for the child with a drinking problem.

With this arrangement, Larry and Edie were quite comfortable in knowing that they had protected an inheritance for all *three* of their children.

To recap, most folks opt to have their children serve as the trustees of their own SAFE Trusts, so they can be in control. But sometimes that's not the best option. If you have a child that's a spendthrift, or has a substance-abuse problem, or has mental or emotional deficiencies, or is under the thumb of a spouse you don't trust, using a Managed SAFE Trust may prove to be the safest way to pass on an inheritance.

SPECIAL NEEDS SAFE TRUST

Being responsible for a child or other loved one with disabilities or special needs is an exceptional experience. But it also creates special responsibilities, which may last for your entire lifetime and beyond. And it usually calls for special legal planning.

You may be able to provide for your child's needs now. But what will happen when you're gone? Who will watch out for your child? Where will your child live? Where will the money come from to support him or her? Could your child qualify for public benefits? You must prepare a plan that provides answers to each of these questions.

I work with parents of disabled children frequently, and although parents are quick to say they would not trade the responsibility, they worry deeply about the future. Planning for a child's life after you're gone is essential, and a Special Needs SAFE Trust is often the primary tool.

WHO SHOULD WATCH OUT FOR YOUR CHILD?

There's no easy answer. The first place to look is to other family members, often your other children. But before naming another child as the caregiver, make sure that person understands the undertaking and is willing to accept all the responsibilities. And you have to decide if you feel comfortable with the plan, even if they're willing. As you know, this is not done lightly.

Where else can you look besides children or other family members? A few social service agencies will provide your child with care and supervision. These are often affiliated with religious groups (such as the Lutheran Ministry and the Jewish Family Services Association).

HOW SHOULD YOU HANDLE THE INHERITANCE?

When it comes to money, there are typically two key issues: management and public benefits.

Can your child handle money? If the answer is no, leaving him an inheritance outright won't make any sense.

Is your child currently on public benefits, or will the child become eligible in the future? If so, you can't simply leave money directly to your child. Eligibility for many benefits—such as Medicaid (health coverage), Supplemental Security Income (SSI), and food stamps—depends on a person's assets and income. An inheritance almost certainly would put your child above the allowable limits and preclude him or her from receiving those public benefits. Let's take a look at why leaving an inheritance directly to a child with special needs can be a very bad decision.

Lisa's Story

At his death, Roy left his disabled thirty-two-year-old daughter $200,000. Roy hoped this money would supplement the Medicaid and SSI benefits she was receiving. Even with these benefits, she had significant additional financial needs.

Unfortunately, the inheritance caused Lisa to lose her Medicaid and SSI benefits, because the state said she had "too much money." Over the next several years, Lisa's inheritance was swallowed up by her hospital and medical bills. When her inheritance had been entirely exhausted, she regained the Medicaid and SSI eligibility. But then there was nothing left of Roy's money for Lisa's food, clothing, rent, and other needs that were not covered by public benefits.

SHOULD YOU LEAVE THE INHERITANCE TO ANOTHER PERSON?

This is one option. But it's usually not a very good one.

Let's say you have two children: a son who is healthy and a daughter with a disability. You could leave your daughter's share of the inheritance to your son and hope he uses it for your daughter's benefit. But this is very risky, even if your son is a trustworthy, loving boy.

If your son is later divorced, or if he dies before your daughter, some or all of the money you intended for your daughter's benefit may wind up with your son's spouse. She may not be as willing to use the funds for your daughter. And if your son has an auto accident, or a business reversal, and is sued, his claimant or financial creditor could wind up with your daughter's inheritance.

WHAT'S A BETTER SOLUTION?

For most people, the best option will be to set up a Special Needs SAFE Trust (also called a Supplemental Needs SAFE Trust). This starts out as a standard Revocable Living Trust. While you're alive, the assets are completely yours.

At your death, the assets you intend to leave for your child with special needs will go into a SAFE Trust for your child. But this one's a little different from the SAFE Trusts we've discussed so far. The regular SAFE Trust or Managed SAFE Trust typically will cause your child to lose eligibility for needs-based public benefits, such as Medicaid or Supplemental Security Income (SSI). A Special Needs SAFE Trust, on the other hand, can preserve your child's eligibility for public benefits.

While there are several options, the most common Special Needs SAFE Trust is the Discretionary Special Needs SAFE Trust. In this case, the funds in the Special Needs SAFE Trust could be used to help pay for your child's needs during his lifetime. The assets in the trust would *not* throw your child off of public benefits. Instead, the inheritance you left would be there to supplement his benefits. And that's important, since public benefits cover only the most basic of a person's needs.

At the death of the disabled child, any funds left in the Special Needs SAFE Trust would go to others in the family (rather than to the state). To accomplish that, you must give the trustee *complete discretion* over when and how to spend (or not spend) the money in the Special Needs SAFE Trust during your disabled child's lifetime. This is the key feature of the Discretionary Special Needs SAFE Trust.

Let's say you leave $100,000 in a Discretionary Special Needs SAFE Trust for your daughter, giving the trustee complete discretion. Your daughter will keep her public benefits, and the trustee may use funds in the trust to cover costs not paid by the government. If over her lifetime, half is used for her needs, then at her death, the remaining half can pass to people you've designated, perhaps your daughter's children or siblings.

The drawback of this type of trust is that the trustee has complete discretion. The trustee can decide whether to use funds in the trust for your disabled child, *or not*. The trustee can't use funds for himself or others—at least not directly. But if the person you select to serve as trustee is also a beneficiary at your child's death, which is often the case, you've built in a dangerous conflict of interest. The trustee might hold back funds to your child, in hopes that he'll get more after your child dies. If you don't think that can happen, think again.

Lucy's Story

Lucy has Down's syndrome. When her mother, Celia, died, Lucy received a $300,000 inheritance in a Discretionary Special Needs SAFE Trust. Lucy's brother Rob was named as trustee and beneficiary at Lucy's death.

Lucy could live on her own as long as Rob watched out for her, managed her finances, and paid her bills. Lucy was living in a subsidized apartment and used Medicaid as her health insurance.

Lucy worked part-time as a dishwasher in a public school cafeteria. She made almost nothing. Her apartment was barely habitable, located in a run-down part of town. Rob could have used money from the trust to help her move to a nicer, safer locale, but he chose not to. Lucy wanted to take vacations with a friend, but Rob put stiff caps on where she could go and how much she could spend.

Rob claimed he was simply being prudent, trying to stretch Lucy's inheritance. But she wasn't even receiving all the income, so the trust fund just grew. It certainly seemed like Rob's decisions were being influenced not by what was best for Lucy but by the fact that he would be the beneficiary after she passed away.

Even if your trustee is not a beneficiary, there are still plenty of risks when you give the trustee broad discretion. If the trustee takes a very restrictive view of what your child may receive, your child may suffer. If the trustee gets angry with your child for some reason, he could "punish" your child by holding back funds. If you are thinking of giving the trustee broad discretion, make sure you *carefully* select the trustee, and talk to the person you select as trustee to make sure he or she will understand your goals and intentions for your child. We'll talk more about selecting a trustee in Chapter 7.

CELIA'S REVOCABLE LIVING TRUST
WITH A STANDARD SAFE TRUST FOR ROB AND
A DISCRETIONARY SPECIAL NEEDS
SAFE TRUST FOR LUCY

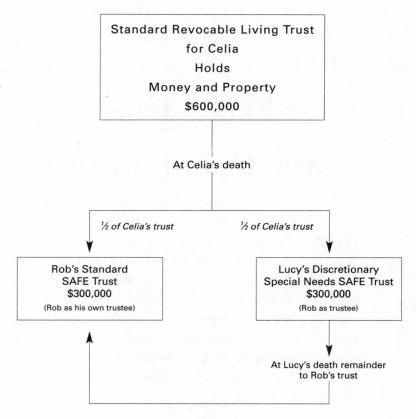

A Discretionary Special Needs SAFE Trust offers critically important protections for your disabled child. This enables your child to receive any public benefits he/she would otherwise be entitled to, and your inheritance can be used to enhance your child's quality of life by supplementing those benefits.

CHAPTER 6

Safeguard
Your Estate from
Three Common Traps

SAFE Trusts are wonderful tools designed to protect the inheritance you leave for your children (and others) after you die. But sadly, in many cases inadequate planning means that your estate could be depleted before anything ever reaches your heirs. What can dissipate your estate? The most common traps are second marriages, lawsuits, and nursing home costs. A comprehensive SAFE plan will not only protect your children after receiving the estate, but it will also help ensure the estate will get to them at all.

Trap 1: Second Marriages

Here's the problem: At your death, you'd like to leave your estate both to your spouse and, later, to your kids. While your spouse is living, you want him or her to benefit from your assets, remain at home, receive income from your investments, and maybe even tap the principal of the investments as well if

THE PROBLEM WITH LEAVING EVERYTHING TO THE SPOUSE

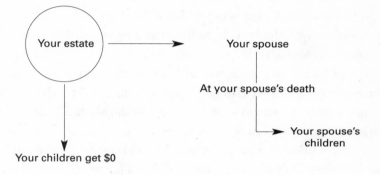

necessary. But you don't want to leave your assets directly to your spouse, because you're afraid your kids might never receive anything.

Why not? Perhaps your spouse is not very good at managing money. Or your spouse may have a gambling, drug, or alcohol problem and be likely to squander the inheritance.

Or this may be a second marriage, and your children are from your first spouse. If you leave your estate to your new spouse, outright, he may later leave the assets only to *his* family, cutting your kids out.

On the other hand, leaving your estate immediately to your children at your death (directly or into SAFE Trusts for them) is not the right solution either, because that would cut your spouse out completely. Is there a solution for you?

The answer is: Use a Marital Starter Trust (also sometimes called a Q-TIP Trust), combined with a SAFE Trust. With Marital and SAFE Trusts, you can have the best of both worlds: your spouse can benefit during his or her lifetime, but your kids will also be protected. Here's a case showing how it works:

The Case of Mary and Joe

This was both Mary's and Joe's second marriage. Although her marriage to Joe was a happy one, Mary had children from a prior relationship, and she wanted to make sure they were fully protected.

With this in mind, Mary set up a Marital Trust, and she put her home and investments (which she brought to the marriage) into it. The total value of her estate was $800,000, but that really doesn't matter. It could have been $80,000, or $8 million. She served as her own trustee, and she maintained complete access and control. At her death, according to her wishes, one of her children would take over as trustee, to manage the Marital Trust. She could have named anyone, even her second spouse, Joe, but she chose her son.

After considering what she wanted to allocate for her spouse, Mary provided in her Marital Trust that her husband Joe would have the right to live in the home for his life, as long as he paid all the expenses, including maintenance, utilities, and taxes. (Some folks limit the period to a year or two.) She also gave Joe all the income (interest and dividends) generated from the trust investments. She decided not to allow him any of the principal, though she could have. Some spouses give the surviving spouse a fixed "allowance," perhaps $1,500 a month, which may come from income and principal (if the income alone isn't sufficient). Others choose to give the spouse access to principal for specified needs, such as food, clothing, shelter, and health care, but not entertainment, travel, and other luxuries.

Joe has only those rights specifically provided by the terms of Mary's Marital Trust. Joe can't take more from the Marital Trust than the trust allows. If Joe gets remarried, he can't take money for his new wife. If Joe gets remarried and then divorced, his wife can never claim assets in Mary's Marital Trust.

At Joe's death, the assets remaining in the Marital Trust pass into the SAFE Trusts for Mary's kids. Joe cannot direct these funds to his own children. This arrangement achieves Mary's goals of providing for her husband while protecting her children.

Note: While there's rarely a problem with one spouse putting her separate investments into a Marital Trust, the home (and other real estate) may be more difficult. That is because, in most states, once the marriage

MARY'S MARITAL TRUST
COMBINED WITH SAFE TRUSTS FOR HER CHILDREN

Mary is trustee and has complete access and control

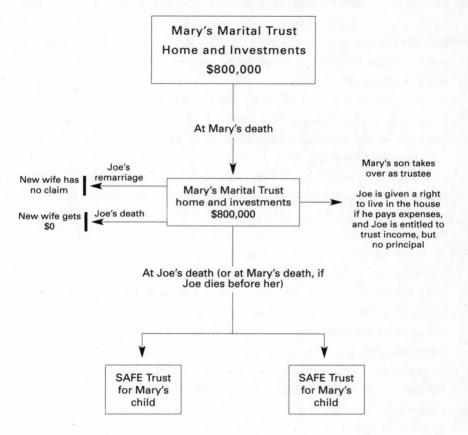

Mary's Marital Trust
Home and Investments
$800,000

At Mary's death

Joe's remarriage → New wife has no claim

Joe's death → New wife gets $0

Mary's Marital Trust
home and investments
$800,000

Mary's son takes over as trustee

Joe is given a right to live in the house if he pays expenses, and Joe is entitled to trust income, but no principal

At Joe's death (or at Mary's death, if Joe dies before her)

SAFE Trust for Mary's child

SAFE Trust for Mary's child

Bottom Line: Mary's husband benefits and her children are protected.

occurs, both spouses gain ownership rights in real property. In the case of Mary and Joe, Joe willingly signed off on his property rights, allowing Mary to put the house into the Marital Trust.

There's another protective benefit to this Marital Trust/SAFE Trust combination arrangement too: death tax savings. Let's take the case of Polly.

Polly's Case

Polly died in 2004, leaving an estate of $3 million. If she had left it all to her kids immediately upon her death, and bypassed her husband Sanford, $2 million would have been exempt from federal death tax; the remaining $1 million of her estate would have created a tax for the kids of just over $400,000. But by leaving at least $1 million in a Marital Trust for Sanford, Polly was able to eliminate those estate taxes by "using" Sanford's exemption from the federal death tax.

In this case, Polly left $2 million immediately into SAFE Trusts for her kids, while leaving the other $1 million to remain in a Marital Trust for her husband. By doing this, Polly was able to forward some money to her kids immediately at her death, while protecting some benefits for her husband. In addition, the $2 million left to her children's SAFE Trusts was within Polly's $2 million exemption from federal death taxes, so there was *no tax* to pay on those assets at the time of her death. And there was *no tax* on the Marital Trust at Polly's death because it was left for her husband's benefit.

After Sanford dies, the remaining $1 million (or whatever's left in the Marital Trust) will pass into the SAFE Trusts for Polly's kids. Those dollars will pass free of federal death taxes too (up to the amount of the exemption, which presently is $2 million), because at Sanford's death the Marital Trust will apply against Sanford's own federal death tax exemption. (Keep in mind that Sanford's estate for tax purposes will include the assets in Polly's Marital Trust *plus* his own assets.) In other words, by dividing her estate as she did, Polly may have made her kids wait a little longer for the remainder of their mother's funds (until Sanford dies), but they actually will come out ahead, saving a lot in federal death taxes. In this case, the savings is likely to be $400,000! Everyone wins: Polly wins, because her goals are fulfilled. Sanford wins, because he gets the use of the income from $1 million during his lifetime. And even Polly's kids win, because they save $400,000. The only "loser" in this scenario is Uncle Sam, and I don't think you'll feel too sorry for him.

Marital Trusts have become increasingly popular in recent years, perhaps because so many people are remarrying after the first spouse dies or gets divorced. With a Marital Trust and SAFE Trust combination, you can protect your loved ones in a fair and equitable manner.

POLLY'S MARITAL TRUST
COMBINED WITH SAFE TRUSTS FOR POLLY'S KIDS

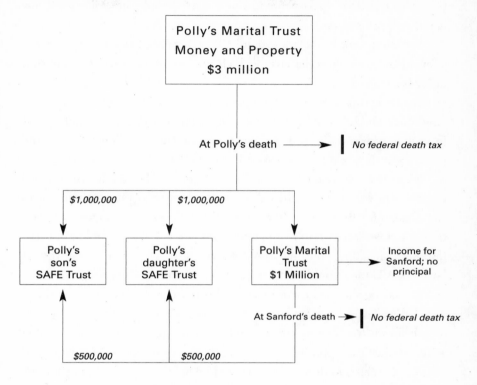

Bottom Line: Polly's husband and children all win, and Polly's wishes are fulfilled.

Trap 2: Lawsuits

Tornadoes, hurricanes, terrorist attacks, catastrophic illnesses—these dreaded images are the ones likely to come to mind when we think of disasters. Odds are that lawsuits would never even appear on your "worry radar screen." Yet the fallout from being sued could obliterate your life savings just as dramatically as any natural disaster. Standard Revocable Living Trusts cannot protect your assets from lawsuits and creditors. And while SAFE Trusts can protect your children's inheritance once you've gone, they don't protect your life savings while you're alive.

The likelihood of a lawsuit is a whole lot greater than a tidal wave passing through your living room. The unfortunate but true reality is that we live in a litigious society. The most common floods come not from water but from the flood of lawsuits in our courts. People sue for almost any harm, real or imagined.

You think your life is "watertight"? Think again! Let's take a look at just a few of the possible situations in which your entire life savings could suddenly be washed away.

Your dog runs away, and before you can track Fido down, he bites your neighbor's child. You thought you had taken reasonable precautions by fencing in your yard. Your dog had never caused any problems before. And it turns out the child had provoked Fido by teasing him.

Many states have adopted the "one free bite" rule, which basically says dog owners will not be held liable for the first time their animal harms someone; after that, the owner is on notice of potential danger and is required to take steps to protect people from the dog. But a number of states impose financial responsibility on pet owners the very first time anyone is harmed. A lawsuit could take a big bite out of your bank account.

Or maybe the mail carrier slips and is injured on your snow- and ice-covered walkway. In some states, failure to take reasonable steps to clear a path for visitors may result in liability for the property owner. In other states, it's just the opposite: by clearing the walk of snow but inadvertently leave an icy patch underneath, you could be held liable for creating a more dangerous condition! One slip and your savings could slip away too.

You're engaged in a conversation with a group of acquaintances. When the name of Mrs. Smith comes up, you make the offhand remark that her husband's a thief. Unfortunately, one member of the group is a friend of the Smiths and reports the comment. Mr. Smith sues you for slander. Guess who will have the last word?

What if your son lends his bike, skateboard, or Jet Ski to a friend, who rides it recklessly and is injured. *You* could be sued and, possibly, held liable.

Or perhaps a trespassing neighborhood child jumps the fence around your backyard and drowns in your pool or pond, or hurts himself falling down a hole. Don't be surprised if you're hauled into court in these situations.

A criminal grabs your purse and tries to run off with it. You fight back, and in the process, you break the criminal's jaw. The next thing you know, he's suing you! Who ever said crime doesn't pay?

Maybe you're an accountant, attorney, or financial adviser, and one of your partners or employees commits malpractice. You might find yourself dealing with a massive court judgment—against you!

Do you own any rental property? Perhaps after buying a new residence you couldn't sell your existing home, so you rent it out. One of the tenants is injured when the railing on the stair breaks, or during an electrical fire. And guess what? You are liable! You could watch your life savings go up in smoke.

Anyone can be sued. Some judges have been adopting more creative theories of liability, and in some cases juries have been willing to render huge judgments.

We've already talked about how the SAFE Trust can protect your *children's* inheritance from *their* lawsuits and creditors. Now let's ask: Is there any way to protect your own assets, during your lifetime, from lawsuits and creditors? Fortunately, the answer is yes.

Everyone needs to consider taking steps to protect their assets from lawsuits. The most important protection comes from liability insurance. Individuals should make sure they have a good home owner's or renter's policy and comprehensive automobile coverage. Property owners should carry liability protection, and professionals (e.g., doctors, lawyers, accountants, financial advisers) should purchase malpractice protection.

And in many cases, people should purchase an "umbrella" policy, which typically increases their liability coverages under home owner's and auto policies by an additional $1 million or more.

Although insurance is necessary, it may not be sufficient to protect you completely; no matter how much insurance you have, you could be sued for more. If you have $300,000 coverage, you may be liable for $500,000; with $1 million of insurance, you could be liable for $2 million.

And your liability policy may exclude coverage for certain events. For example, if you are sued for an "intentional" wrongdoing, like slander or libel, your policy probably won't pay. Ask a trusted insurance agent to review your liability risks and to recommend appropriate coverages.

Then there's the issue of the reliability of the liability insurers themselves. Some companies have gone out of business, leaving policyholders stranded in a sea of lawsuits.

To help bulletproof your assets, you can do more than just purchase insurance. There are also a variety of legal tools that are available to enable you to place your life savings beyond the reach of a lawsuit. Please understand, lawsuits do serve an important role when correctly used, allowing injured victims to recover just compensation from wrongdoers. But as explained above, Americans today run the risk of being held liable for injuries for which they were not really at fault. Your entire savings may be stripped from you, though you personally did nothing wrong, at least not intentionally. Recognizing this potential for unfairness, legislators and judges have created techniques to allow Americans to protect themselves against the litigation explosion.

There are a variety of legal asset-protection tools available. They range from simple to pretty sophisticated, from low-budget to expensive. One of these tools or some combination might be appropriate. For many folks, the best response will be a Creditor Protection Starter Trust combined with a SAFE Trust. To help you better understand how these legal protections can help, let's take a look at the most popular techniques.

- *Transfer to a Spouse.* Maybe the simplest asset-protection solution for a married couple is to transfer assets to the spouse least likely to get sued. If *you* are sued for an auto accident, or for malpractice, or as a property owner, *your* assets are exposed, but your spouse's generally are not. Of course, if you put everything into your spouse's name, and then your *spouse* is sued, you made a costly mistake. And you'll be giving your spouse a practical advantage if he/she files for divorce after you've moved everything to his/her name. If your estate is over the federal estate tax limits, moving everything into a spouse's name may cost your heirs quite a bit at death. And if one spouse dies and leaves the assets to the surviving spouse, that undercuts the original protections, because after the survivor gets the inheritance, that spouse's creditors can grab the inheritance.

- *Gifts to Adult Children.* No one can take what you don't have. So making gifts to adult children (or others) protects those assets from your creditors. This may be easy, but keep in mind it is also risky. Will your children hold the assets for you and return them as you need them? Are you sure? And if your child divorces, dies, or is sued, "your" assets may wind up in the hands of your child's ex-spouse or creditors.

   Some experts suggest reducing the risk, at least with real estate, by retaining what is called a "limited or special power of appointment." This gives you the right to change the recipient of the gift (other than to yourself). Let's say you give property to your son, Bob. If he later decides to get divorced, or is himself sued, you can take the ownership of the property from him and transfer it to his sister, Susan. This technique carries some risk, because its use has not yet been widely affirmed by the courts.

- *Homestead.* You may move to one of several states, most notably Florida or Texas, and buy a home there. These states protect a residence, regardless of its value, from lawsuits and creditors. Only a home gets this special protection.

- *Life Insurance.* Many states protect life insurance products, including annuities, from lawsuits. In these cases, any cash surrender value in the policy is protected while you are alive, and the death benefits cannot be grabbed by your creditors at death. But there is one significant exception, one creditor that's *not* barred from grabbing your life insurance. Can you guess who? Of course, it's the IRS.

- *Pension Benefits.* Creditors cannot seize assets in a retirement plan qualified under the federal Employee Retirement Income Security Act ("ERISA"). This protection generally applies to 401(k), defined benefit, profit sharing, employee stock ownership (ESOP), stock bonus, and Keogh plans. This protection under ERISA does not apply to an Individual Retirement Account (IRA), a Simplified Employee Pension (SEP), or a Savings Incentive Match Plan for Employees (SIMPLE), though many states have adopted their own laws protecting these retirement accounts. The federal bankruptcy laws provide protections for IRAs, SEPs, and SIMPLEs, but you must file for bankruptcy, which has serious ramifications. If your state does not currently protect IRAs, think twice before rolling your ERISA-protected company retirement plan into an IRA.

- *Limited Liability Companies (LLCs).* You've probably heard that many businesses incorporate to protect the owners' personal assets from liabilities of the business. With LLCs (and Limited Partnerships), individuals can obtain a similar type of shield for personal savings, investments, and real estate.

    Here's how they work. You create a Limited Liability Company by signing legal documents. You then move the assets you wish to protect by titling them into the name of the LLC. The LLC gets its own tax identification number (like a Social Security number) and files a separate income tax return. But that's usually very simple.

    An LLC actually gives two types of protections from lawsuits: First is personal protection. If you are personally sued for something you supposedly did, such as an auto accident, your assets in the LLC are protected. The second protection is for lawsuits arising from assets in an LLC. Let's say you created an LLC to hold a two-family rental property, and one tenant is hurt in an electrical fire. The renter, if successful in a lawsuit, can only go after your LLC assets (the rental property). But the renter cannot grab any assets not in that LLC, such as your home, personal bank accounts, and other investments.

PROBLEMS WITH THESE CREDITOR-PROTECTION TOOLS

All these creditor-protection tools provide benefits, but none is perfect standing alone. For example, as I've noted, putting assets into a spouse's name is easy, but may be a mistake if your spouse is the one who is sued, if your spouse files for divorce, or if your total estate exceeds the federal death tax exemption.

Gifts to adult children are risky, because you lose control. When your kids have your estate, watch out!

You can buy a home in Florida or Texas, but that won't help if you don't choose to live there. Life insurance and retirement plans get automatic creditor protection, but you certainly don't want all your life savings in those limited vehicles.

Limited Liability Companies are pretty good, but they're not perfect. For example, if you put your home into an LLC, you may lose the income tax breaks that normally follow home ownership (e.g., the ability to deduct mortgage interest payments). And you won't get the SAFE Trust protections for your children at your death (unless you put the ownership of the LLC units into a Revocable Living Trust combined with SAFE Trusts for the heirs).

Is there a better alternative? In many cases, the best protection may be a Creditor Protection Trust combined with a SAFE Trust. Let's see what extra benefits this option offers.

CREDITOR PROTECTION/SAFE TRUST COMBINATION

The Creditor Protection Trust and SAFE Trust combination is very different from the standard Revocable Living Trust combined with a SAFE Trust.

In most states, a Revocable Living Trust, with you serving as your own trustee and giving you the broadest access to the assets placed in the trust, provides *no* protection whatsoever from *your* creditors and lawsuits. At your death, the kids can get protection from *their* creditors and lawsuits through the SAFE Trusts, but while you are alive, there is no protection for *you* from your own creditors and lawsuits.

Recently, in response to the litigation explosion, a few states around the country—including most notably Alaska, Delaware, Missouri, Nevada, and Rhode Island—have adopted laws allowing you to set up a Creditor Protection Starter Trust with your own assets, for your own benefit, while also protecting the assets from the reach of lawsuits and creditors. You can set up a Creditor Protection Trust under the law of these states even if you don't live, or have never set foot, in those states. (Creditor Protection Trusts are relatively new, and some experts remain skeptical about the effectiveness of these trusts and are waiting to see if judges will enforce the lawsuit protections.)

Each state has adopted its own set of specific requirements that must be met. For example, under Alaska law, you may retain the right to revoke or terminate the Creditor Protection Trust, but only with the consent of another person who has a substantial interest in the trust. In Delaware, the Creditor Protection Trust must be irrevocable. Delaware law generally allows you to have a power to veto an independent trustee's decisions to make distributions from the trust, and although you will name the beneficiaries when you set up the trust, you may retain the right to change them. You may name some other person (whom you trust) who can advise the trustee to act on your priorities (e.g., to give you income and even principal from the trust).

Even though you don't have to live in the state providing your Creditor Protection Trust with these valuable protections, you typically need some connection. At least some of the assets should be deposited in accounts in that state, and your trustee (a person or institution) should be located in that state.

With the Creditor Protection Trust, you can give yourself a present and enjoy the same wonderful protections from lawsuits and creditors that you will give your children under a SAFE Trust.

LAYERING PROTECTIONS

Just as you might layer your clothes on a frigid winter day to provide an extra measure of protective insulation, you can do the same with your legal wardrobe to boost its protective powers. Using multiple tools may be wise. For example, you might place much of your assets into a Limited Liability Company, and place the ownership of the LLC into your spouse's Creditor Protection Trust. This layers on three separate protections: picture yourself putting your warm flannel shirt on when you place the assets into your spouse's name; next comes the sweater over the shirt, when your spouse places the assets into an LLC; and then the LLC goes inside the Creditor Protection Trust, the warm, down-filled overcoat. The more layers of protective clothing, the more likely your savings will be kept warm and safe.

The Case of Tracy and Alvin

Alvin was a physician. He had been sued twice, but both lawsuits were frivolous, and his insurance company had never had to pay a cent. But having

TRACY'S CREDITOR PROTECTION TRUST COMBINED WITH SAFE TRUSTS FOR THE KIDS

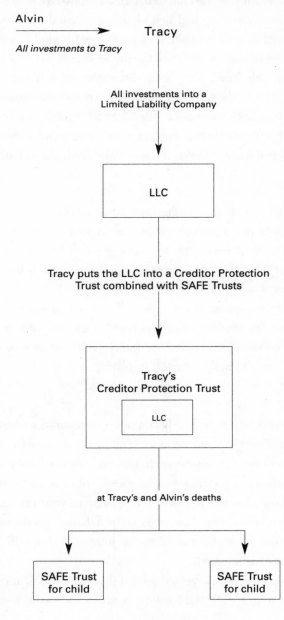

been sued, Alvin was nervous about the possibility of future lawsuits; one day a jury might rule for a sympathetic patient even if Alvin didn't do anything wrong. Alvin's wife, Tracy, was an at-home mom; the odds of her being sued were fairly slim, so the couple decided to move Alvin's investments into Tracy's name. Since they had been happily married for twenty years, Alvin felt comfortable with the shift. Tracy set up a Limited Liability Company to hold the investments, and then the ownership of the Limited Liability Company was titled into Tracy's Creditor Protection Trust. At Tracy's death, if Alvin was alive, the Creditor Protection Trust could provide income to Alvin. And when both were gone, the Creditor Protection Trust would distribute to SAFE Trusts for the children. This arrangement allowed Alvin and Tracy to sleep at night, thanks to the multilayered protection.

TIMING

Procrastination is not only the thief of time, but it can be the thief of money too. If you wait until you're sued, *none* of these asset-protection techniques will work. In fact, you may only protect your assets *before* you are even on notice of a claim. You cannot use these tools to hide assets from present or threatened lawsuits or you may be committing fraud.

In addition, you should never move all of your assets under one of these plans. First, it's prudent to always have quick and easy access to at least some part of your estate. And second, by law you cannot use these asset-protection tools to make yourself insolvent.

AFTER A LAWSUIT

Once you've been sued, immediately contact your insurance carrier, which should provide a lawyer for your defense. If you've been sued for more than the insurance coverage, you may need to hire your own attorney as well.

If a lawsuit ends in a judgment that exceeds your insurance limits, and you have not taken adequate protection to safeguard your estate, you may need to consult a bankruptcy lawyer as well. A bankruptcy will typically wipe out your existing debts, including the judgment, but will leave you very little of your existing assets.

The time to plan is now, *before* the legal floodgates open and you have been sued. Building a watertight estate is no job for a do-it-yourselfer.

Without expert help, your savings are likely to be washed away. So get on your life jacket and consult with an attorney who is experienced in keeping people afloat with asset-protection planning.

Trap 3: Nursing Home Costs

The biggest threat to the financial security of most older Americans and their families is the catastrophic cost of long-term care, particularly nursing home care. This pronouncement is not marketing hyperbole recited by business-hungry insurance agents or lawyers hoping to scare up new estate-planning business. It's simply a true, sad reality. The late U.S. Congressman Claude M. Pepper, who was a leading advocate for senior citizens' rights, also recognized that "the single greatest fear of our senior citizens, and of all Americans, [is] that a long-term catastrophic illness may strike and, because of the absence of public or private coverage, they will become destitute."

No one wants to go into a nursing home, and no spouse or child wants to put the other spouse or parent into a home. But sadly, there may come a time when there's no choice. Nursing homes around the country are overflowing with folks who never wanted or intended to be there.

Nursing home care is expensive. While the costs vary around the country, annual costs of $60,000 to $80,000 are quite common. More than a million Americans every year become victims of health care impoverishment, having been forced to give up their homes and life savings to pay the bills for long-term care.

Medicaid is the only program that will pay for a long-term stay in a nursing home. Not Medicare, not Social Security. We hear a lot about the importance of Medicare and Social Security and not much about Medicaid. Yet Medicaid is as important as Social Security and Medicare.

Medicaid is a crucial safety net for the poor and middle class. For most older Americans, it's the only thing standing between some semblance of financial security and total financial devastation. Yet despite its importance, Medicaid is treated like the Rodney Dangerfield of federal programs: It just "gets no respect." One need only observe Uncle Sam's rapid response to the devastation of Hurricane Katrina in 2005 and the contrast becomes apparent. After the weather disaster, our politicians quickly responded to the human crisis, promising billions of dollars in special relief funds for New Orleans and affected states. They determined, correctly, that the federal government has an important obligation to come to the aid of Americans who, because of an act of God, not any fault of their own, lost their homes. Medicaid plays the same role—it is disaster relief for older Americans and their families who, because of no fault of their own, have become critically or chronically ill and now face the total loss of their homes and life savings. Yet Medicaid is all too often painted as a handout to the undeserving. This is puzzling, because, as you'll see, eligibility for this program is far from easy.

Medicaid will cover long-term care in a nursing home. But there's a hitch, and it's a big one. To qualify, a person must either be or become poor. You cannot have much money or property to qualify for Medicaid. Disaster relief for hurricane victims is *not* conditioned on a person's having little or no money and property, but Medicaid is.

For a married couple, the government takes a "snapshot" of all the assets owned by the couple (with a few exceptions, discussed later) on the date of "institutionalization." Institutionalization is the date one spouse leaves home, to enter either a hospital or a nursing home (or both) for an extended period without returning home. Medicaid counts assets in the name of the husband, wife, joint between husband and wife, and even most assets jointly held with the kids. In most states, the couple must "spend down" half of the total, but may keep no more than $99,540 (2006). In some states, the couple may keep $99,540 even if that's more than half.

While $99,540 isn't much, that's the good news. The bad news is that a single person (widowed, divorced, or never married) is only allowed to keep about $1,500 to $5,000, depending on the state.

There are also a few "exempt" assets, items that the government says are so important that you're allowed to keep them. For example, you are allowed to keep your household goods, personal effects, and clothing. Uncle Sam won't force you to sell the shirt off your back. You can keep burial plots and prepaid funeral contracts too. Your life insurance policies with a face value of $1,500 or less are also protected.

Two other important exemptions: The family home (with equity up to $500,000 or $750,000, depending on the state) is exempt as long as one spouse is living there. That protects the home for a married couple but doesn't do a thing for single folks. (And even for married couples, upon death many states will grab the home and sell it to recoup the Medicaid benefits previously paid.) One car is exempt for a married couple, regardless of its value. A single person may only keep a car with a value up to $4,500. (I don't know what our legislators are driving!)

By now you should get the point: The government doesn't make it easy to preserve much of your nest egg if Uncle Sam is footing the bill for your nursing home care. But don't despair just yet.

The Medicaid rules allow folks to take affirmative steps to protect more of their life savings. You have to *do* something, though; the benefits are not automatic, as they are under Social Security and Medicare. Under Medicaid, the law allows you to protect a portion of your life savings by taking action like moving available assets into exemptions, giving assets to children, and setting up specialized trusts. This works more like the death tax rules, under which people have to take affirmative (legal) steps to keep more of their savings for their family and away from Uncle Sam.

One of the most common planning strategies is to give assets to children (or other family members). The law allows you to put your home, cash, and other investments into the names of your kids in order to protect them from the nursing home.

Now, you can't just write a check to your children, pull your pockets inside out, walk into the Medicaid office, and expect coverage. Almost every gift or transfer of assets will trigger a waiting period (also called an ineligibility period, or penalty period) for Medicaid benefits. While it's perfectly legal to give away your savings, you will have to wait until the ineligibility period runs out before coverage will kick in.

The rationale behind this wait is not unreasonable: the government figures that individuals and families should pay a fair share of their long-term care costs. But it's Uncle Sam's concept of reasonable that causes major trouble for folks.

Calculating the ineligibility period is complex. The length of time you'll have to wait to get benefits after making a transfer will depend on the amount of the transfer. Each state sets an "average cost of nursing home care," usually ranging from $4,000 to about $7,000 per month. These amounts change regularly, so check with your local Medicaid office for current rates.

To figure the ineligibility period, look at any gifts or transfers within the last three years (for gifts made prior to February 8, 2006) or five years (for gifts made on or after February 8, 2006, or at any time if made to or from a trust). This three-year (or five-year) period is called the "look-back" period. Transfers made beyond the look-back period are free and clear, and don't have to be considered.

For gifts made within the look-back period, divide the value of the gift by the average cost of nursing home care set by your state. Let's assume that the average cost of care is $5,000 a month. A $10,000 gift creates a two-month period of ineligibility for Medicaid ($10,000 ÷ $5,000 = 2 months). A gift of $100,000 creates a twenty-month period of ineligibility.

For gifts/transfers made prior to February 8, 2006, the ineligibility period begins to run from the first day of the month in which the gift was made (or the following month in some states). For gifts/transfers made on or after February 8, 2006, the ineligibility period begins to run from the date that you both apply for Medicaid and would be eligible for benefits but for the gift.

If you gifted $100,000 in May 2005, that gift would make you ineligible for Medicaid for twenty months (beginning in May or June, depending on the state). You'd be ineligible for Medicaid through December 2006 (or January 2007). Assuming you met the other Medicaid rules, you could qualify for benefits beginning the following month.

Let's take a look at another example. If you made a gift of $300,000 in May 2005, you would have made yourself ineligible for Medicaid for sixty months (until May of 2010), assuming a $5,000 average cost of care. But if you wait three years, until June of 2008 to apply for Medicaid, the $300,000 would be free and clear. That's because the penalty period for gifts and transfers made before February 8, 2006, only applies to transfers made within the three-year look-back period immediately prior to the application.

One more example: You have total savings of $100,000, and you have entered a nursing home because of mobility problems. You now (after

February 8, 2006) give away $50,000 to your children (creating a ten-month Medicaid ineligibility period) and purchase an immediate Medicaid-qualified annuity designed to pay you enough monthly income (along with your Social Security) to cover almost all your nursing home charges for the next ten months. Your Medicaid application is denied for ten months, but when that period expires you become eligible for Medicaid benefits.

Gifting or transferring assets can be a wonderful tool to enable you to protect a portion of your savings, for your spouse's or family's needs, in case you require nursing home care. Because of the existence of the penalty periods for transfers, the earlier you move assets to the kids, the more you may be able to preserve.

Now comes the problem: Giving assets to your kids is very risky. Lots of folks move their home and the bulk of their savings into the children's names to protect the assets from nursing homes and Medicaid, all the while thinking (hoping?) that the kids will allow them to continue living in the home, and will give them cash back as they need it. And you know what? Sometimes that's just how it works. But sometimes things go wrong, very wrong.

If you transfer assets over to your kids, the children become the legal owners. This means that once the children have their names on the house title, they can change the locks and kick you out. And there's nothing you can say. If you ask for money to buy a new car, they can tell you that your old car runs just fine (even though it has 150,000 miles on it). If you would like to take a vacation and need cash, they may suggest you stay home instead to conserve money for your old age (which really means saving it so there will be more left for an inheritance).

And it's not just your children that you have to worry about. You may have the best, most loving, most trustworthy children in the world. But what if your children get divorced? Half of your money and property could wind up with the spouses. Try to get the money back then!

What if your child dies? Chances are, his or her will leaves everything to the spouse, again leaving your security in serious jeopardy. And if your child dies and leaves your assets to his children who are still minors, they *cannot* legally give you any money back, even if they wish to do so.

Your child could get sued, perhaps because of a financial reversal or an auto accident. It doesn't matter how loving and loyal your child is. If she hits a carload of kids and injures them, *your* money (in her name) could quickly disappear.

Finally, you also need to worry about the tax laws. Gifting can cost you a lot in added taxes.

No, I'm not talking about gift taxes. You can give away $12,000 per person per year (and your spouse can do the same thing) without paying any gift tax, and without even filing any return. But you can also give away $1 million in your lifetime, over and above the $12,000 annual gifts (and your spouse can do the same thing), without either you or your children paying any gift tax, though you will have to file a gift tax return. The return is just informational. As long as your estate is less than $1 million, $2 million if married (and most folks who engage in Medicaid planning are well below these figures), you can give your entire estate away at one time to one person with no tax to you or to the recipient.

No, it's not usually gift tax that you have to worry about. But you do have to consider potential capital gains taxes if you give away appreciated assets, such as your home.

Appreciated assets are those that have gone up in value since you first purchased them, and often include stocks, antiques, and real estate (including your home). Capital gains taxes are charged on profits made when anything that has increased in value is sold. The initial purchase price (the "basis") is not taxed—only the increased value, the profit, is taxed. Capital gains tax rates are generally 15 percent. The rate is 5 percent if the seller's income is less than $30,650 (single) or $61,300 (married). These amounts are as of 2006.

Forgetting Medicaid and gifting for a moment, there are two ways that you can avoid paying capital gains tax. First, for a home, if you owned your residence for at least two years prior to selling it, you can sell and avoid paying any capital gain tax on up to $250,000 of the gain or profit ($500,000 if you're married). This special tax break applies only to your home, not investment real estate, and not stocks, antiques, or other assets.

The second way to avoid capital gains tax is to hold the appreciated asset until your death. At your death, appreciated assets passing to your heirs get a "stepped-up" basis, which basically means that the capital gains tax is eliminated. For example, if you bought stock years ago for $10,000, and it's now worth $110,000, you'd pay $15,000 of tax if you sold it during your lifetime (15 percent of the $100,000 profit). But if you hold it until death and leave the stock to your kids, and then the stock is sold for $110,000, they pay *no* capital gains tax.

Now back to Medicaid and gifting. If you give away appreciated assets to your children during your lifetime, they *don't* get either of these tax breaks. If your children sell the home after you move it into their names, they'll pay capital gains tax on the profit, because it's not *their* residence. They own it but don't live there. The profit is calculated on *your* basis (purchase price). So, for example, if you bought your home for $50,000 and give it to your children, then they later sell it for $300,000, they'll pay capital gains tax of $37,500 (15 percent of the $250,000 profit).

Your death also does not provide any tax break with respect to appreciated assets given away during your lifetime. If you give appreciated assets to your children, including a home and anything else, they'll pay capital gain tax on the profit when they sell (even if they wait to sell until after you die), again based on your basis. If you paid $10,000 for your stock, and your kids sell it for $110,000 (either before or after you die), they'll pay $15,000 capital gains tax (15 percent of the $100,000 profit). Your death would not give them any special tax break.

One more tax to worry about: the income tax. When you own an investment that generates income (a CD that produces interest, or a mutual fund that produces dividends), you pay income tax. When you give the assets to the kids, they don't pay income tax on the receipt of the investment (the CD or mutual fund itself), but *they* (not you) will pay income tax on the income generated after they're the owners. And if they earn more than you, their income tax rates may be higher than yours.

For example, let's say you transfer $100,000 in cash to your son. Your son pays no income tax when he receives the money. He then invests the cash in CDs yielding 4 percent—$4,000 in annual interest. That interest is added to his work income and will be taxed, just like any other interest income he receives from investments. At his rates, he may pay $1,400 of tax on the income (35 percent of $4,000). At your tax rate (15 percent), you would have paid only $600.

So what does this all mean? If you do nothing, your heirs may wind up with nothing. Gifts/transfers can be an important planning tool to enable you to protect your home and a portion of your life savings from catastrophic nursing home costs. But giving away your home and even a part of your savings to your kids can be very risky. And there may be added capital gains and income taxes.

The critical question becomes: Is there any way to protect assets from the nursing home and avoid these risks and taxes at the same time? Thankfully, the answer is yes: You would first start with a Medicaid Trust, and combine it with SAFE Trusts to protect your children.

A Medicaid Trust is quite a bit different, and more restrictive, than a plain vanilla Revocable Living Trust (or most other Starter Trusts). To work, a Medicaid Trust must meet three primary rules:

1. The trust must be irrevocable and unchangeable during your lifetime. Once set up, you can't ever change your mind or the terms of the trust.

2. You can have no control over the assets in a Medicaid Trust. Neither you nor a spouse, if applicable, may serve as the trustee. You can pick a child or anyone else, but the trustee cannot be you or a spouse.

3. You can never touch the principal placed in the Medicaid Trust. You can (and usually would) retain the right to *income* produced by these assets, and you would provide in the trust that upon your death these assets would go into SAFE Trusts for your children. But you may not remove or receive any of the principal deposited into the trust.

Putting assets into an irrevocable Medicaid Trust triggers the same look-back and ineligibility rules as gifts directly to children or others on or after February 8, 2006. And transfers into a Medicaid Trust require that you give up control over the assets, just as you do with gifts directly to children or others. But you may still talk to your child who is serving as trustee, and you may make suggestions about how to handle investments in the trust. And there are lots more protections. Even if a child is serving as trustee of a Medicaid Trust, assets in the trust do not belong to the child—he or she cannot legally take the funds and run off to Tahiti or otherwise spend them on himself or herself. If a child becomes divorced or dies, the assets remain in the Medicaid Trust—they do not pass to the child's spouse or children, or even into the kids' SAFE Trusts. As long as you live, the assets remain in your Medicaid Trust, paying the income to you. Let's look at an example.

Bob's Case

Bob set up a Medicaid Trust and SAFE Trust, putting his home and about $100,000 of investments into the Medicaid Trust. His daughter, Julie, was the trustee of the Medicaid Trust. According to the terms of the trust, Bob kept a legal right to live in the house, so Julie could not throw him out under any circumstances. He also kept a right to all the income from the trust investments. The $100,000 produced $4,000 a year of income, which Julie was required to pay to Bob.

A few years later, Bob decided to move to an apartment. Julie was required by the trust language to sell the home and invest the funds, still within the Medicaid Trust. She took the $100,000 of sale proceeds, invested those in more CDs, and paid the entire $8,000 a year of interest to her dad.

More than five years after the assets were placed into the Medicaid Trust, Bob needed to enter a nursing home. At that time, the $200,000 of assets in the Medicaid Trust were protected. He continued to get the $8,000 of income, which was paid to the nursing home, along with his Social Security and pension, but Medicaid paid the $60,000 annual balance. At Bob's death, the entire $200,000 in the trust was safely passed to Julie's SAFE Trust.

Putting assets into a Medicaid Trust/ SAFE Trust combination can protect your money and property, while eliminating many of the problems of gifting directly to kids.

The children may have control as trustee, but their control is restricted. They can't throw you out of the house, and they can't refuse to pay you the income produced by the investments. You can't touch the principal (the property or the investments) that you put into the Medicaid Trust, but for most people that's not a hardship, because they weren't cashing in CDs or stocks to pay bills. Most folks need the *income* from their investments to live on, and that's what can be guaranteed for you by the Medicaid Trust.

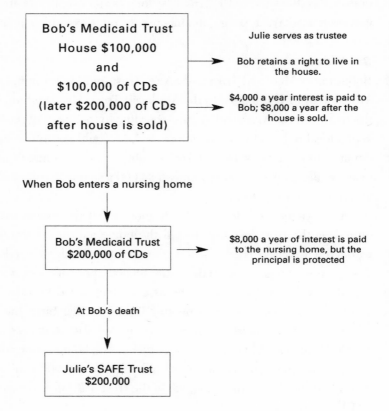

Bob's Medicaid Trust
House $100,000
and
$100,000 of CDs
(later $200,000 of CDs
after house is sold)

Julie serves as trustee

Bob retains a right to live in
the house.

$4,000 a year interest is paid to
Bob; $8,000 a year after the
house is sold.

When Bob enters a nursing home

Bob's Medicaid Trust
$200,000 of CDs

$8,000 a year of interest is paid
to the nursing home, but the
principal is protected

At Bob's death

Julie's SAFE Trust
$200,000

With a Medicaid Trust, you'll get the income, for sure. If you just give your savings over to your children directly, without a Medicaid Trust, there's no guarantee you'd receive anything!

In addition, if your child gets a divorce, the spouse can't touch the assets in the Medicaid Trust even though your child is serving as trustee of the trust. If your child dies, the assets in the Medicaid Trust stay there, generating income for you. They don't pass to your child's spouse or kids, or into the SAFE Trusts, while you are alive. If your child is sued, his/her creditors can't touch the assets in the Medicaid Trust.

What about taxes? A Medicaid Trust protects you and your family there too. In the example above, Julie sold the home while Bob was alive. Thanks to the magic of the Medicaid Trust, there was no capital gains tax on up to $250,000 of profit ($500,000 if Bob was married). And if the house remained in the Medicaid Trust without being sold until after Bob died, there would be no tax on *any* of the gain/profit—even over $250,000. After Bob was gone, the home could have been sold, and all the proceeds, without reduction for capital gains taxes, would have passed into the SAFE Trust for Julie.

And don't forget that you gain all the standard benefits of the SAFE Trusts: protection after you're gone for the kids in case they get a divorce, or when they die, or if they're sued. If you just give assets outright to the children to protect your money and property from nursing home costs, the assets are theirs. You've lost all the future SAFE Trust protections and receive no assurances that your assets will ever reach those whom you hoped would benefit from your life's labors.

PART III

Creating Your SAFE Plan

CHAPTER 7

Crafting a Comprehensive Solution-Driven Strategy

When you go to Burger King, you could buy just a hamburger. Or a milk shake. Or French fries. But lots of hungry folks pick a combo meal because it includes everything they want in one neat package. You can do the same thing with the SAFE strategies we've been discussing (and without all the fat and calories too!), incorporating multiple planning strategies to address multiple needs. And you can get exactly what you want and need.

We've talked about more than a dozen different types of problems and solutions. Many of the planning solutions start with a Starter Trust, typically a simple Revocable Living Trust to avoid probate. Then instead of leaving your estate directly to your children at your death, you leave the kids' inheritances into SAFE Trusts.

As we have already discussed, there's not just one type of SAFE Trust. (See below the chart summarizing SAFE Trusts and Starter Trusts.) You can do a Managed SAFE Trust for a

SUMMARY OF SAFE TRUSTS

SAFE TRUSTS	PRIMARY BENEFITS
STANDARD SAFE TRUST	Protects your child's inheritance from your child's spouse in a divorce. Protects your grandchild's inheritance from your child's spouse after your child dies. Protects your child's inheritance from his/her creditors and lawsuits. Maintains privacy for child's inheritance.
DYNASTY SAFE TRUST	Extends SAFE Trust benefits for multiple generations.
CRUMMEY SAFE TRUST	Provides SAFE Trust protections for gifts made during your lifetime.
DEATH TAX PROTECTION SAFE TRUST	Protects your child's inheritance from taxation at his/her death.
RETIREMENT FUND SAFE TRUST	Extends income tax deferral for retirement funds left for your child or grandchild, while providing standard SAFE Trust protections for those funds.
MANAGED SAFE TRUST	Provides financial management for a child who is young or immature and cannot manage money.
SPECIAL NEEDS SAFE TRUST	Provides management for a child with special needs, while protecting the child's public benefits.

SUMMARY OF STARTER TRUSTS

STARTER TRUSTS	PRIMARY BENEFITS
STANDARD REVOCABLE LIVING TRUST	Protects your estate from the costs, delays, and hassles of probate at your death, while allowing you to keep control during your lifetime.
A-B TRUST	Avoids death taxes on up to $4 million for married couples.
LIFE INSURANCE TRUST	Avoids death taxes on life insurance proceeds.
CHARITABLE TRUST	Maximizes income and tax benefits for you, while helping your favorite charity.
MARITAL TRUST	Provides benefits for your spouse (second marriage) while protecting your children's inheritance.
CREDITOR PROTECTION TRUST	Protects your assets during your lifetime against creditors and lawsuits.
MEDICAID TRUST	Protects your home and life savings if you must enter a nursing home.

child who will need help managing the inheritance. A Special Needs SAFE Trust is important for a child with a disability. A Retirement Fund SAFE Trust provides wonderful income tax benefits when you own an IRA or other retirement account. A Crummey SAFE Trust is a useful way to make gifts to family members while keeping the gifts away from the in-laws. A Death Tax Protection SAFE Trust can protect your children from paying death taxes when they pass away. A Dynasty SAFE Trust can provide the protections, not just for your children but for grandchildren, great-grandchildren, and on down your family bloodlines.

And you don't have to start with a simple Revocable Living Trust. You may use SAFE Trusts with a variety of Starter Trusts, including A-B Trusts (to protect your estate from *your* death taxes), Marital Trusts (to allow your spouse to benefit from your estate, while still protecting your blood heirs), Life Insurance Trusts (to keep life insurance proceeds from taxation), Medicaid Trusts (to shelter your estate from nursing home costs), and Creditor Protection Trusts (to protect against lawsuits and creditors).

What if you have multiple concerns, as many people do? Can you use more than one of these trusts? Guess what? You don't have to pick just one. In many cases, it makes a lot of sense to combine several strategies in one SAFE estate plan, and sometimes even in one document.

Let's look at several examples of how this works.

The Case of June

June has three children: Bob, Stan, and Laurie. Stan and Laurie are both healthy and doing quite well. But Bob has serious mental and emotional problems and will not be able to live on his own. Right now, Bob's living with his mom, and she's caring for him. But when June's gone, she's hoping either Stan or Laurie will step in to help.

June has wisely combined a standard Revocable Living Trust as her Starter Trust with standard SAFE Trusts for Stan and Laurie and a Special Needs SAFE Trust for Bob. Here's how it works:

While June is alive, she remains in complete control of her estate. Though she retitled her home and savings into the name of her Revocable Living Trust, she remains the trustee.

When June passes away, she wants half of her estate to be held for her son Bob, and the other half to be split between Stan and Laurie. It's not that she likes Bob more—it's just that Stan and Laurie are doing fine financially, while's Bob's financial needs will be far greater.

Bob can't get his inheritance outright for two reasons. First, he couldn't manage it. He really doesn't understand money and finance. And second, he may qualify for public benefits in the future. June recognizes that living on public benefits won't give Bob much of a life, so she would like the inheritance to be available to supplement any government programs for which Bob may qualify.

COMBINATION TRUSTS: REVOCABLE LIVING TRUST DISTRIBUTING TO STANDARD SAFE TRUSTS AND A SPECIAL NEEDS SAFE TRUST

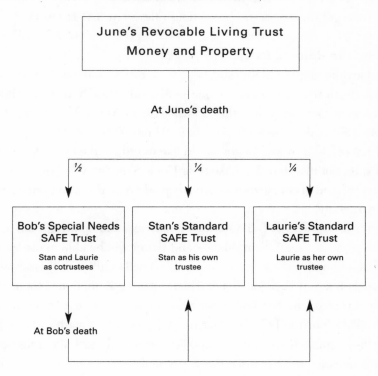

June serves as her own trustee

June's Revocable Living Trust
Money and Property

At June's death

½   ¼   ¼

Bob's Special Needs SAFE Trust

Stan and Laurie as cotrustees

Stan's Standard SAFE Trust

Stan as his own trustee

Laurie's Standard SAFE Trust

Laurie as her own trustee

At Bob's death

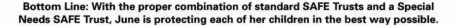

Bottom Line: With the proper combination of standard SAFE Trusts and a Special Needs SAFE Trust, June is protecting each of her children in the best way possible.

June wisely set up her estate so that when she's gone, Bob's inheritance will pass into a Special Needs SAFE Trust. Stan and Laurie will serve as cotrustees, with very broad discretion as to how to manage Bob's inhertance and when to use the funds for his benefit. June trusts Stan and Laurie to do the right thing for their brother. If there's anything left when Bob dies, then the remaining funds would pass to Stan and Laurie.

Stan and Laurie are both married, and June has a nice relationship with their spouses. But she also realizes that lots of folks get divorced these days, and June wants to make sure her children are protected. So she creates regular SAFE Trusts for the inheritances to be received by Stan and Laurie. They shall serve as their own trustees, so they'll have control, but they'll also get the wonderful protections offered by SAFE Trusts.

Mandy and Roger's Story

This married couple has an estate of just under $7 million, well over the federal death tax exemption for one individual. They have two children, one who's a doctor and the other a businessman. While both kids are just getting started, they are both likely to build nice estates of their own.

First off, Mandy and Roger would like to reduce the estate tax at their deaths. It's not that they don't like their Uncle Sam, but why pay more than necessary? And of course they've already paid tax on this money once when they earned it.

By starting with A-B Trusts for themselves, and splitting their assets about evenly between them, Mandy and Roger will be able to use each of their $2 million death tax exemptions, allowing $4 million of their estate to pass to their kids with *no* death tax. The remaining $3 million of their estate will be taxed to the tune of about $1.4 million, leaving a total of about $5.6 million for their kids. Without the A-B Trusts as a starter, Uncle Sam could have grabbed an extra $900,000 (because only $2 million instead of $4 million would have escaped the death tax)!

They like the SAFE Trust protections for both of their children, particularly the creditor/lawsuit protections. Their daughter Carole is a doctor, and although radiology is not the highest-risk health care specialty, the lawsuit protections would give them peace of mind. Their son Alan is an entrepreneur, and even Donald Trump has gone through rough times. Again, the creditor protections of the SAFE Trust would assure their son that he'd never be completely without any financial safety net.

If the children are financially successful, they'll be able to accumulate nice estates of their own. Both are very responsible with money. Mandy and Roger decided that it would make sense to combine the regular SAFE Trusts with Death Tax Protection SAFE Trusts (see Chapter 4) so their kids

COMBINATION TRUSTS: A-B TRUSTS DISTRIBUTING TO REGULAR SAFE TRUSTS AND DEATH TAX PROTECTION SAFE TRUSTS AND DYNASTY SAFE TRUSTS

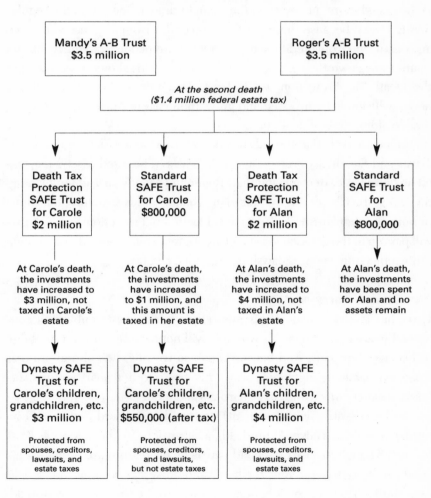

Mandy's A-B Trust
$3.5 million

Roger's A-B Trust
$3.5 million

*At the second death
($1.4 million federal estate tax)*

Death Tax Protection SAFE Trust for Carole $2 million

Standard SAFE Trust for Carole $800,000

Death Tax Protection SAFE Trust for Alan $2 million

Standard SAFE Trust for Alan $800,000

At Carole's death, the investments have increased to $3 million, not taxed in Carole's estate

At Carole's death, the investments have increased to $1 million, and this amount is taxed in her estate

At Alan's death, the investments have increased to $4 million, not taxed in Alan's estate

At Alan's death, the investments have been spent for Alan and no assets remain

Dynasty SAFE Trust for Carole's children, grandchildren, etc. $3 million

Protected from spouses, creditors, lawsuits, and estate taxes

Dynasty SAFE Trust for Carole's children, grandchildren, etc. $550,000 (after tax)

Protected from spouses, creditors, and lawsuits, but not estate taxes

Dynasty SAFE Trust for Alan's children, grandchildren, etc. $4 million

Protected from spouses, creditors, lawsuits, and estate taxes (at their deaths) wouldn't have to pay estate tax on up to $4 million of the inheritance from their parents.

So the two kids will each inherit about $2.8 million, with $2 million going into a Death Tax Protection SAFE Trust (which is the most that the tax law allows to go into this trust) and $800,000 passing into the regular SAFE Trust. When the kids have expenses, these trust funds will be the *last* monies they should use. First, they should spend their personal funds that are not in any SAFE Trust, because those funds get no special protections. If they need more money, then they should draw money from the regular SAFE Trusts, because those get the protections from a spouse at divorce and death, and from creditors, but do not get protection from the children's estate taxes down the road. The *last* money the kids should spend is from the Death Tax Protection SAFE Trust. That money, Mandy and Roger hope, will simply be invested and grow, then pass to Mandy's and Roger's grandchildren free of death taxes.

Since it's likely that the kids will do well themselves, the regular SAFE Trusts and Death Tax Protection SAFE Trusts (if invested wisely) may become quite large. Recognizing that, Roger and Mandy also added Dynasty SAFE Trusts (Chapter 3) to their plan. Thanks to this structure, the assets in both the regular SAFE Trusts and Death Tax Protection SAFE Trusts will pass on to the grandchildren and great-grandchildren—with continuing protections from spouses, lawsuits, creditors, and taxes!

The Case of Larry and Sue

Larry has always managed this married couple's investments. He's concerned that when he dies, his wife Sue will not have the interest or ability to manage the funds. And because Sue's so trusting, he's also afraid that some sweet-talking gigolo will worm his way into her heart and pocketbook, walking away with Larry's hard-earned money.

So Larry (with Sue's agreement) starts with a standard Revocable Living Trust while he's alive. At his death, assets will be held in a Marital Trust for Sue. Though this isn't a second marriage, his reasons are sound. At his death, if he predeceases Sue, the home and brokerage account will be held in a Marital Trust for Sue's benefit. Sue will *not* be the manager. Instead,

Larry is naming his younger brother as his first backup trustee, and then his son Don as the next alternate.

While Sue's alive, she'll be able to live in the home. She's entitled to all the investment income. And she can even receive principal from the Marital Trust if the trustee decides she needs it. But since she's not in charge, the funds are protected for her from future boyfriends or husbands. At Sue's death, the remaining assets will go into the SAFE Trusts for the kids.

Larry also has an IRA with about $200,000. In most cases, the best approach is to name the spouse as the primary beneficiary. But if Larry does

COMBINATION TRUSTS: REVOCABLE LIVING TRUST, STANDARD SAFE TRUSTS, AND RETIREMENT FUND SAFE TRUSTS

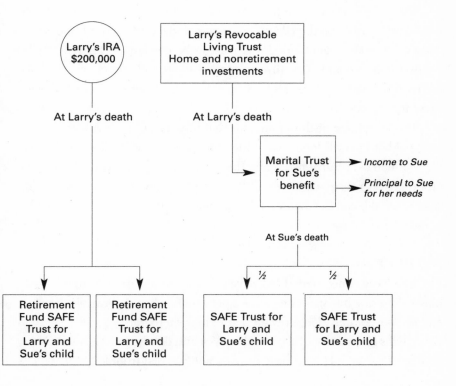

that and dies first, then Sue would get those funds outright. And they'd be fair game for Sue's future handsome gigolo.

Larry could leave the IRA funds to the Marital Trust. But the income tax would not be the most favorable. Sue's Marital Trust would receive minimum distributions from the IRA based on her life expectancy. But when Sue died, the remaining IRA funds would have to be disbursed to the SAFE Trusts for the children over the rest of Sue's "theoretical" life expectancy.

For example, let's say when Larry died Sue's life expectancy was fifteen years. One-fifteenth of the IRA would be paid into her Marital Trust the first year, one-fourteenth the next year, and so on. If Sue then died twelve years after Larry, she's have three remaining years on her "theoretical" life expectancy, and those IRA funds would all be distributed within the next three years. The children would lose the benefit of an extended payout of the IRA over *their longer* life expectancies, which would cause them to lose a tremendous income tax benefit.

The couple agreed that Sue would have plenty to live on from the investments apart from the IRA. So Larry created a Retirement Fund SAFE Trust for the kids, and named that trust as beneficiary on his IRA. At his death, the house and nonretirement investments will be held in the Marital Trust for Sue, and the IRA will pay into the Retirement Fund SAFE Trust for the children.

The advantage of this strategy is that instead of the IRA having to be fully paid out over fifteen years (Sue's life expectancy), it can now be paid out one-half over thirty-five years (the elder child's life expectancy) and the other half over thirty-eight years (the life expectancy of the younger child). And as we showed in Chapter 4, the longer the payout, the greater the tax benefits.

Phyllis's Case

Phyllis is very concerned about paying her entire estate over to a nursing home. She saw her sister's estate evaporate after her sister broke her hip, and she desperately doesn't want that to happen to her.

Phyllis has one son, Jim, and she loves him dearly. But he is something of a ne'er-do-well. He's a heavy drinker, and has had trouble holding a job.

Not surprisingly, he constantly has financial problems. But he's Phyllis's only child, and he's actually been quite attentive to her.

Phyllis is a healthy eighty-five-year-old. She is not comfortable putting any of her assets into Jim's name for fear his creditors could grab them. But she understands that if she keeps the assets and winds up in a nursing home, her son could get nothing.

So Phyllis has established a Medicaid Trust combined with a Managed SAFE Trust. She put the house and her savings into the Medicaid Trust as her Starter Trust. She has the right to live in the home for life, so no one can throw her out. And she must be paid the interest and dividends from her investments. It's not all that much, perhaps $10,000 a year, but that plus her Social Security and pension is the money she lives on. She can no longer take out the CDs and mutual funds from the Medicaid Trust, but she doesn't need to. As long as she still gets the income, she'll be just fine.

COMBINATION TRUSTS:
MEDICAID TRUST DISTRIBUTING TO
MANAGED SAFE TRUST

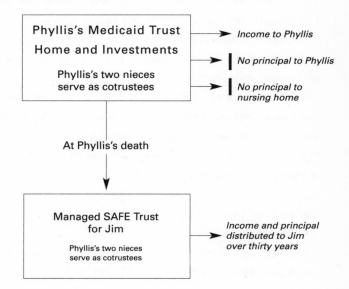

Phyllis isn't comfortable naming her son as trustee, and with a Medicaid Trust Phyllis can't serve as her own trustee. While she knows her son wouldn't do anything to harm her, his drinking scares her and she's just not comfortable putting him in charge.

Her sister has two kids, and both are responsible adults. They also are close to Phyllis. So Phyllis has named them as cotrustees.

The Medicaid Trust assets will be protected for her son, even if Phyllis has to go to a nursing home. At her death, given Jim's drinking problems, she doesn't want the assets to go directly to him or to name him as trustee of the SAFE Trust. In a drinking binge, he might drain all of its funds. Phyllis wants the funds to last for Jim's lifetime.

So Phyllis created a Managed SAFE Trust for Jim that names her two nieces as trustees. She doesn't want Jim to browbeat them for money, and she doesn't want to put them in an awkward position. So Phyllis does not give them any discretion over the distribution of the assets from Jim's Managed SAFE Trust. Instead, they are instructed to pay him equal portions of the trust over the next thirty years. Now Phyllis can rest more comfortably, knowing that Jim will have a source of income for thirty years after she passes on.

These are just a few of the many trust combinations that you may utilize. Each type of Starter Trust and SAFE Trust has benefits. Just like the family-style meal at a Chinese restaurant, you may pick one from column A, one from column B, and one from column C. And when you're done, you've created a delicious banquet of benefits that suits the personal taste of you and your family.

But coming up with comprehensive solutions to your concerns and problems involves much more than simply picking from trust plans. There are many other pieces to the planning jigsaw puzzle. And if any piece gets lost, your plan may never fit together properly. The eight "pieces" that most often get overlooked are:

- Picking the proper trustees.
- Making sure your estate avoids probate.
- Deciding when it may be *better* to spend your estate through probate.
- Making sure you properly address the "little" items in your estate.

- Ensuring that your estate goes to the right people.
- Helping your heirs find your assets.
- Updating your SAFE plan.
- Bulletproofing your plans against challenges.

SELECT THE RIGHT TRUSTEE

Most of the SAFE planning arrangements discussed so far begin with a Starter Trust that you can control (e.g., Revocable Living Trusts, A-B Trusts, and Marital Trusts). If you're like most folks, you want to be in control of your money and property for as long as you can. That makes perfect sense. But there may come a time when you'll no longer be able to handle your financial affairs: certainly when you die, and possibly if your health renders you unable to manage for yourself.

You must plan ahead by naming alternate trustees to take over for you in the future. The decision as to whom to select is critically important. Remember, while you're alive but incapacitated, this person will be managing your money for you, with the power to take funds from your bank accounts, sell your mutual funds, even sell your home. And at your death, this is the person who will oversee your trust, pay the final bills, sell assets if appropriate, and then allocate the remainder to the SAFE Trusts for your kids.

With a few Starter Trusts, including the Life Insurance Trust, Medicaid Trust, and Creditor Protection Trust, you can never serve as your own trustee. In those cases, you must select another person as trustee right from the start.

Then there's the matter of naming trustees for your children's SAFE Trusts. This decision may actually be more important than the selection of alternate trustees for your Starter Trust. I say this because your alternate trustees only take over when you are no longer able to handle your affairs, and the alternate trustee's job may only last a year or two. The story is very different for your children's SAFE Trusts, where the trustees will serve for your progeny's entire lifetimes and perhaps longer.

As a result, the considerations are different, depending on whether you are selecting an alternate trustee for your own Starter Trust or selecting trustees for your children's SAFE Trusts. So we'll discuss each separately.

ALTERNATE TRUSTEES FOR YOUR STARTER TRUST

So back to the question: Who should you pick as trustee for your own Starter Trust if you cannot serve in that capacity? Perhaps it may be better to first answer the question: Who should you *not* pick? Lots of folks make costly, painful trustee selection mistakes. Here are the top six.

Trustee Error 1: Don't Pick a Child Just Based on Birth Order

Most folks pick the spouse first, if married, and then a child. That often makes sense. But which child should you pick? Instead of selecting the most capable, lots of folks pick the eldest.

Being the eldest doesn't make your child smarter, more responsible, or more trustworthy. In fact, age doesn't make your child anything but older. If everything else is equal, then pick your oldest. But everything else rarely is equal. And if that's the case, go for honesty, common sense, and compassion.

Trustee Error 2: A Local Trustee Isn't Necessarily Better

Many people pick a child or other relative who lives nearby, even if that person is not the best choice.

It's nice to have a trustee handling your finances who's in town. But that shouldn't be the most important factor. Most important is trust. If you live in Virginia, but the person you trust more than anyone else is your brother in California, pick him. In this age of computers, e-mail, fax machines, and overnight delivery, long distance isn't very distant anymore!

Trustee Error 3: Knowing About Money Isn't Everything

Again, it's nice to have a trustee with a Ph.D. in business and finance. But remember, trustworthiness is most important. If you have the choice between a financial genius who may steal your money, and a trustworthy child who doesn't know what a mutual fund is, go with the trustworthy child. He or she can always hire a financial adviser to help.

Trustee Error 4: Don't Pick a Trustee with Personal Financial Problems

This probably seems obvious, but it's a mistake that occurs far too often. If a person has had trouble managing his own money, why would he be any better able to handle yours? You wouldn't think of putting a box of candy in front of a diabetic who loves sweets. So why give a person with personal financial problems easy access to and control over your money and property? You might be creating a temptation your trustee can't resist.

Trustee Error 5: Don't Select a Trustee with a Spouse You Can't Stand
Spouses have a way of influencing each other. If you give your son control over your finances, will his self-centered wife (whose motives you don't trust) become involved? Would you want your son's wife having a say, even indirectly, over your money and property? Think about that before naming a trustee.

Trustee Error 6: Don't Pick Cotrustees Who Can't Get Along
Your son and daughter are like the Battling Bickersons—they never agree on anything. Then why in the world would you name them as cotrustees of your trust? If you think this appointment will bring them together, forget it. If they don't get along now, they won't get along when it comes time for them to act for you later.

All right, so now that I've told you who *not* to pick as trustee of your Starter Trust, let's answer the question: Who *should* you select?

When choosing someone to manage your trust, ask yourself:

- Do you have complete faith in the person? Serving as a trustee requires integrity.
- Is the person willing to accept the job? Just because you name someone doesn't mean he or she will accept. Talk it over first, and outline the responsibilities.
- Where does the person live? It needn't be a major problem if your trustee is out of state; but for convenience's sake, the closer to home the better.
- Would it be better to name an institutional trustee than a family member? If the management of the trust is complicated and an appropriate family member isn't available, consider naming a professional trustee, such as a financial institution. On the downside, banks are impersonal and charge annual management fees typically ranging from

½ of 1 percent to 1 percent of the value of the trust's assets. They may also be unwilling to handle any trust with total assets of $100,000 or less. On the upside, an institutional trustee is accustomed to the responsibility, and it has a deep pocket to cover any losses due to theft or other mismanagement.

As mentioned earlier, a trustee is a powerful position, and giving someone power over your finances carries risk. Picking a trustworthy trustee is the best way to limit the risk. But if you're not entirely comfortable with naming one person as trustee, you may consider picking two or more cotrustees who must act together. For example, you may provide that all three of your children will become cotrustees, to act by majority or unanimous vote. Two or three would have to sign the paperwork to withdraw funds from your accounts or sell your home. As cotrustees, your kids would only be able to steal from you if they work together! But naming cotrustees places an added burden on your kids—and if they don't get along, this can exacerbate the problems between them.

TRUSTEES FOR YOUR KIDS' SAFE TRUSTS

When you create a SAFE Trust, you must select the trustees and alternate trustees who should manage your children's inheritance after you are gone.

As discussed in Chapter 3, you may choose to name your children as their own trustees, or you may name a third party to manage for them (Chapter 5). Most folks choose to allow their kids to manage for themselves, because they don't want their children to have to ask someone else for their inheritance money.

If your kids are responsible adults, they should be able to manage for themselves. But if they lack that attribute, or if they have a drug, alcohol, or gambling problem, or if they can't hang on to money, or if they are so influenced by a controlling spouse that your funds might be diverted—in any of these cases, you should consider naming someone other than your child as trustee of your child's SAFE Trust.

But the decision-making doesn't end there. This trust will last for your child's lifetime. At some point, your child will no longer be capable of managing the SAFE Trust for himself. He or she may become incapacitated, and your child surely will pass on someday. Who should be the alternate to your child to take over for him?

Again, there are two primary considerations: trustworthiness and family dynamics. Here are the most common choices for SAFE Trust trustees, either primary (if not your children) or alternates:

- *Your child's children.* If the child has adult children who have shown themselves to be mature and competent, you may name one of them as alternate. But if your grandchild is only two years old, then he or she is probably not a wise choice, at least not yet. Also if you are picking a grandchild because your child has a drinking problem, or is just irresponsible, consider whether the grandchild will be able to stand up to his parent and say no to requests for money.

- *Your child's siblings.* Many folks name one or more of their other children as alternate trustees for a child's SAFE Trust. Here's where family dynamics may cloud the picture. If your kids don't get along, then don't make one an alternate trustee for the other.

    Let's say your son and daughter don't see eye-to-eye on anything and never have. Naming your daughter to manage your son's assets for him can only lead to trouble. He probably will resent the vote of "no-confidence" that comes with your decision to appoint someone else, no matter who that person is, but naming his sister would be like rubbing salt in a wound. Another factor to consider when naming a child's sibling as an alternate trustee is whether this will damage relations with any nephews or nieces.

- *Your child's spouse.* Yes, I know, a primary purpose of the SAFE Trust is to keep the assets away from the child's spouse. And if you hate the child's spouse, don't name the spouse as the alternate trustee. But keep in mind that the terms of the SAFE Trust can restrict the trustee's use of the funds for your child and grandchildren only, not for the spouse. If the spouse reaches into your child's SAFE Trust and takes funds for herself, in violation of the trust terms, that's theft, and the spouse could go to jail (if she's caught). And the assets in the SAFE Trust are still protected from the spouse in a divorce or at your child's death, even if your child's spouse is trustee. Still, naming your child's spouse is usually a last resort.

- *A financial institution.* Once again, a potential fallback choice is a bank or brokerage firm trust department. There are numerous benefits. An institutional trust department has the knowledge and experience managing billions of dollars of other people's money. And they can and will say no if your children or grandchildren wish to drink, snort, or gamble away the inheritance. On the other hand, an institutional trustee usually just won't have the same compassionate, caring relationship that a family member trustee should have. And an institutional trustee may charge more than a family member for services provided.

- *A mechanism allowing beneficiaries to choose the alternate.* At some point, if the SAFE Trusts lasts long enough, your own choices for trustees and alternates may have moved on to a higher calling. A Dynasty SAFE Trust may last for generations, and there's no way you can preselect specific trustees to handle the trust in fifty years. To cover these cases, your child's SAFE Trust should always include some mechanism for selecting future trustees. A common approach, for instance, would let the beneficiaries of the trust choose their own trustee. Often the beneficiaries will pick another family member of family friend; sometimes they'll select a professional who has worked with the family, or an institutional trustee.

Let's take a look at how one person selected the trustees for his Revocable Living Trust and the children's SAFE Trusts.

Marsha's Story

Marsha established a Revocable Living Trust. There was no question that she would serve as her own trustee. Selecting alternates was pretty easy as well. She named her daughter Ina, because Ina lived nearby and, to be frank, had the closest relationship with Marsha. And if Ina couldn't handle the management, then her son Robert, the financial "expert," would be next.

Robert was an accountant. Though he lived 500 miles away, he was still the next-best choice.

At Marsha's death, the inheritance was to be split equally into three SAFE Trusts, one for each of her three children. Ina and Robert would each serve as trustee of their own SAFE Trusts, because they were capable of handling the money. Ina would serve as Robert's backup, and Robert would be Ina's next trustee. If neither could serve, then Ina's son Leonard would take over for both Ina and Robert.

But Marsha's third child, Tony, was a problem. For years, Tony has had a drug problem. And that has gotten Tony into trouble. He actually spent a couple of years in jail. Since then he has seemed to be getting his life on track. But Marsha was not altogether convinced that he'd be ready to receive a pile of money.

So Marsha named Robert as Tony's primary trustee. She picked Robert because he had a decent relationship with Tony, and because he would

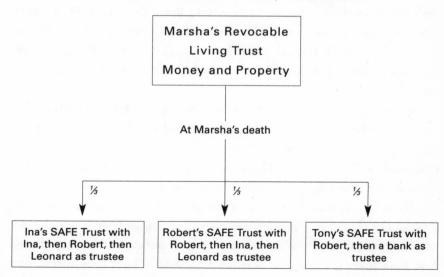

MARSHA'S REVOCABLE LIVING TRUST
COMBINED WITH SAFE TRUSTS FOR THE CHILDREN

Marsha serves as trustee, followed by Ina, then Robert

Marsha's Revocable
Living Trust
Money and Property

At Marsha's death

⅓

⅓

⅓

Ina's SAFE Trust with Ina, then Robert, then Leonard as trustee

Robert's SAFE Trust with Robert, then Ina, then Leonard as trustee

Tony's SAFE Trust with Robert, then a bank as trustee

probably be able to tell if Tony slipped back into drug abuse. If Robert was unable or unwilling to serve, a local bank trust department would become the trustee. She couldn't name Ina, because Ina was a softhearted soul and Tony could too easily manipulate her into doing whatever he wanted with the trust funds.

A Starter Trust for yourself, coupled with a SAFE Trust to protect the children and grandchildren, is a wonderful estate planning tool, offering lots of benefits. But for the trusts to provide the fullest benefits, you must select the right trustees. And that can be a real challenge.

FUND YOUR SAFE TRUST TO AVOID PROBATE

Your Starter Trust combined with a SAFE Trust is designed to avoid probate and obtain a wide variety of protections for you and your family. But your excellent planning will go to waste *unless* you actually *fund* the trust. Funding the trust means that, once you sign the Starter Trust document, you must then place all of your assets, with only a few exceptions, into the trust (imagine putting items into a gift basket or box).

Actually, nothing ever goes into the name of a trust. This is a common mistake people make when funding any trust. A trust can't own assets; only the *trustee* of a trust can own the assets.

I'll clarify how this works. Let's say your name is Ronald Smith and you wish to put your house into the name of your Revocable Living Trust. *Don't* title the house into the name of the Ronald Smith Trust. The proper name to put on the deed is Ronald Smith, Trustee under the Ronald Smith Trust Agreement, dated July 5, 2005 (or whatever the date the trust document is signed).

If you fail to rename assets intended to be placed into the Revocable Living Trust, and those assets remain in your name alone, they can still enter the trust at your death, because the Pourover Will you so cleverly created (see Chapter 8) will put them in. That's helpful. But your estate will go through probate, *unnecessarily,* because a will is not protected from probate.

If you have assets, like a bank account, in your name jointly owned with a spouse or child, or with a spouse or child named as beneficiary, the account will go to the co-owner or beneficiary at your death with no probate. But these assets won't get the benefits of the SAFE Trust. The only way to avoid probate *and* to get the benefits of the SAFE Trust is to put your assets into your Starter Trust as soon as the trust is established, then have the Starter Trust distribute to the SAFE Trusts at your death.

How do you put assets into your Starter Trust? And which ones can't go in, at least not directly? Let's take a look at the most common asset categories.

Cash Accounts

It should be relatively simple to transfer your cash accounts (e.g., savings and checking) and cash equivalents (such as certificates of deposit and money market accounts) into your trust. Just go to the bank or other financial institution where the account or cash equivalent is located and request them to make the transfer. Give them the name of the trust, with the trustee's name first, including the date the trust was signed. They may want to see a copy of the executed trust, or portions of it, and will ask you to complete some paperwork.

Stocks and Bonds

Transfer of bonds, stocks, mutual funds, and similar investment assets may be a little bit more difficult to transfer into your trust, as the paperwork requirements are somewhat more complex. I suggest that you ask your broker or financial planner, if you have one, to assist you with the transfers, as brokerage and other financial firms are familiar with the requirements. If your broker or planner is not willing to assist you, or if you don't have one, you'll have to contact each company in which you own stock, or the transfer agent for the company (often named on the stock certificates), and get the necessary forms for transferring ownership.

If you hold stock certificates yourself, you may wish to take them to a brokerage firm or financial planner and ask them to open an account for the stock; you can have them open the account in the name of the trustee of the trust. That takes the burden off you for changing the name on each stock certificate yourself. Brokers and planners will happily do this work for you, usually at little or no charge. In exchange, you'll use the broker or planner for buying, selling, or managing your account in the future.

Alternatively, your lawyer who established the trust can help with the transfers. The lawyer may charge a fee for this service, so ask him/her what the cost will be *in advance.* You may be able to get the lawyer to help with the funding at no cost in exchange for hiring him to prepare the trust.

Keep in mind: we're talking about transferring the existing stocks into the trust by changing the name of the owner of the stocks. You do not have to sell the stocks first. You can transfer your exact investments into the trust. Selling might cause you to incur a capital gains tax unnecessarily.

Life Insurance

Unless you're doing a Life Insurance Trust combined with a SAFE Trust (see Chapter 4), you generally will not put the ownership of the life insurance into your trust. It's simply unnecessary. But you should name the Starter Trust as the beneficiary.

Life insurance can be confusing because there are three roles for a person (or persons) to play: the owner, the person whose life the insurance is on, and the beneficiary (the person who gets the proceeds at the owner's death). Right now, you're probably the owner, and the insurance is on your life. At your death, the beneficiary is your spouse or kids.

You can't change the person whose life the insurance is on. And there's no need to. The insurance will always pay off at your death. And you don't have to change the owner. It's still *your* policy.

But change the primary beneficiary on *your* insurance to *your* Starter Trust. If your spouse also owns life insurance, he should also change the name of his insurance beneficiary to that of his trust. At your death, the insurance proceeds will automatically funnel into the SAFE Trusts for your heirs, with no probate. And your family will get the SAFE Trusts' protections. Get the change-of-beneficiary form from your insurance agent.

Retirement Funds

Do not transfer the ownership of your IRAs, 401(k)s, 403(b)s, profit sharing, or pension plans to a trust. If you do, the entire account in your retirement fund will be taxed immediately, and you'll get no more income tax deferral, because the tax laws provide that only a person, not a trust, can obtain the tax advantages as owner of retirement funds.

What's the best way to handle your tax-deferred retirement accounts? In most cases, the best plan is to name your spouse (if you're married) as the primary beneficiary, and then your Retirement Fund SAFE Trust as the secondary beneficiary (primary beneficiary if you're not married). The Retirement Fund SAFE Trust was discussed in Chapter 4. This allows your heirs to get the benefits of the SAFE Trust *plus* nice income tax benefits by extending the payout over your child's (or grandchild's) life expectancy.

If you are not setting up a Retirement Fund SAFE Trust, then you may be better off naming your children themselves as the direct secondary beneficiaries. They won't get the benefits of the SAFE Trust, but they will at least get the benefit of extending the minimum required distributions (which provides an income tax benefit).

Real Estate

To put your home or other real estate into your Starter Trust, you'll need to make a new deed for the property. With the deed, you'll be transferring the property from your individual name into the trustee's name.

Remember, this is very important for real estate: a trust cannot own property, only the trustee of a trust can own property. So you'd put the property into the name of the trustee: for example, Mary Smith, Trustee of the Mary Smith Trust Agreement dated March 7, 2005.

Real estaet is the most likely place problems will arise if you do it incorrectly. When you or your heirs go to sell the home, the title company may refuse to issue title insurance (which will upset the sale entirely) if the property had incorrectly been put in the name of the trust itself (e.g., The Smith Trust, instead of Mary Smith, Trustee of the Smith Trust).

If you're setting up two Starter Trusts for you and your spouse, perhaps A-B Trusts combined with SAFE Trusts, you'll have to give special attention to titling the home. Talk to your lawyer about how to hold the home. For example, if you put the home into your spouse's A-B Trust, and she dies first, you could lose the ability to deduct real estate taxes and mortgage interest. And when the property is sold, there's a possiblity that there might be a capital gains tax on the home's appreciation from the time of your spouse's death until the time of the sale.

Car

Put your automobile(s) into your trust. It's really not hard to do. Go to the local title bureau and take a copy of the trust and the car title.

Lots of folks ignore the car, thinking that it will be gone by the time they die. And that's a risk you may decide to take. You may choose to wait until you buy your next car, and just buy that one in the name of the trustee at that time.

But if you take the risk of not putting your car into the trust, and you die, your heirs will be the losers. That's because your car may have to go through probate!

Personal Items with No Title

A bank account has a named owner. So do your stocks, house, and car. How do you put assets into the trust that *don't* have any owner name, like your jewelry, appliances, clothing, and home furnishings?

You may transfer untitled assets into your trust by signing a very simple form, often called a "General Assignment" or "Bill of Sale." This document will say something like "I generally assign all my untitled assets, including my jewelry, household goods, and personal effects, to George Williams, Trustee of the George Williams Trust Agreement dated August 7, 2006."

Checking Accounts

Other than your life insurance, IRAs, and other retirement accounts, the one asset you may not wish to put into the trust is your checking account. This is especially true if your Social Security is being directly deposited into this account. That's because the Social Security Administration doesn't like to deposit checks directly to trust accounts (there's no law prohibiting the deposit of Social Security checks to a trust; it's just the SSA's policy).

If you keep a checking account out of the trust, don't let it get too large. And add a joint owner or beneficiary so that, at your death, the account won't go through probate.

New Investments

As new investments are purchased, it is important that you continue to put the ownership of these assets into your trust. So if you open new bank accounts or purchase new stocks or bonds, the title to the account, stocks, or bonds should be held in the name of the trustee of your trust.

After your Starter Trust is established and funded, you will handle all of your financial affairs through your trust. It's really pretty easy. All receipts of dividends and interest will be received by the trust, and any checks that you would write would be through the trust. (You may establish a new checking account in the name of your trust to facilitate this.)

So long as you are your own trustee, you'll just use your own Social Security number for the accounts in the trust. No employer tax identification number will be needed for the trust, and your individual Social Security number should be furnished to banks, brokers, and others holding trust accounts. No separate federal income tax will need to be filed for the Starter Trust, and all items of income and deductible expenses will be reported on your individual income tax return. While you're alive, nothing changes as far as your taxes go—no pluses, no minuses. You should continue to file your income tax returns as you have in the past.

At your death, a new tax identification number will be required for the trust. That's because your Social Security number no longer can be used—it dies with you. In fact, if there are three SAFE Trusts opened for the three children, each will get its own tax ID number. And there will have to be a separate income tax return done for each SAFE Trust from that point forward. Yes, it's somewhat more burdensome. But the added burdens are well worth the benefits. Trust me.

CONSIDER SENDING YOUR ESTATE THROUGH PROBATE
Earlier (Chapter 3), I explained that when establishing SAFE Trusts, your first step is typically to create a Starter Trust. Then, at your death, the assets pass directly from the Starter Trust into the SAFE Trusts *with no probate.*

This benefit is highly appealing, because as discussed in Chapter 1, probate can be expensive, time-consuming, and a huge hassle.

It's relatively easy to use your Starter Trust/SAFE Trust combination to avoid probate. All you have to do is put your assets into the Starter Trust, naming your trustee as owner of your assets. Then, at your death, the assets distribute into the SAFE Trusts quickly, easily, and inexpensively—with no probate.

In almost all cases you're better off avoiding probate at death. Yet occasionally there's a reason to go through probate. It's rare, but sometimes probate can be a benefit. Let's take a look at the exception to the rule.

When you set up a Revocable Living Trust, you may serve as your own trustee. So far so good. But at some time, you won't be able to continue. At your death, you'll need an alternate trustee to handle the trust, pay the bills, and pass the inheritance into the SAFE Trusts for the kids. And there will need to be trustees for the children's SAFE Trusts.

What if you don't have someone you trust to serve as trustee after you're gone? What if your child isn't capable of handling the trust? What if your grandchildren, other relatives, friends, and even a bank are just not right to serve as trustee?

In that case, the best result might be to have the SAFE Trust go through probate. It's called a Testamentary SAFE Trust. Instead of setting up a Starter Trust that's designed to avoid probate, you would start instead with a will. At death, the will would distribute to a SAFE Trust. Because the estate passes under a will, not a trust, it does *not* avoid probate. In fact, in many states it will stay in probate for as long as the SAFE Trust exists.

Let's say you have one child, and she's just not capable of handling her inheritance after you're gone. You don't want to name a cold, impersonal bank. You have a very small family, and the only other choice is your cousin. But you just aren't absolutely sure that you should trust your cousin with control over your child's inheritance.

When you use a Testamentary SAFE Trust, your child is protected by the probate court. Your cousin will serve as trustee, but in most states the probate court will oversee everything that goes on. Your cousin won't be able to do a thing without the knowledge and approval of the probate court. It makes it a lot harder for the person handling the SAFE Trust (your cousin) to do anything bad or wrong.

Of course, there's a cost to setting up a Testamentary SAFE Trust. Your cousin probably will hire a lawyer to help with the probate court's procedures and paperwork. And the lawyer will want to be paid.

In most cases, it makes sense to avoid probate. But not always. Let's take a look at the case of Wilmer.

The Case of Wilmer

Wilmer had two children, Edina and Patrick. Edina was the apple of his eye, but she was always a little "slow." She never married and had no children. She cleaned houses part-time. Edina always had lived with Wilmer, and Wilmer managed her money. At Wilmer's death, Edina would probably be able to remain in the house on her own, as long as someone paid her bills and managed her funds. The question was who?

Patrick was certainly capable. But Patrick had always been jealous of Wilmer's relationship with Edina, and Patrick felt that Wilmer had already given her way too much money all during her life. Patrick stated that he was willing to help when Wilmer passed on, but Wilmer wasn't entirely sure that Patrick could put aside all the sibling rivalry issues to handle Edina's trust with her best interests in mind.

WILMER'S WILL DISTRIBUTING TO TESTAMENTARY AND STANDARD SAFE TRUSTS

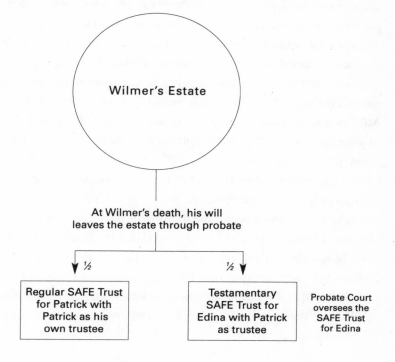

Wilmer's Estate

At Wilmer's death, his will leaves the estate through probate

½ → Regular SAFE Trust for Patrick with Patrick as his own trustee

½ → Testamentary SAFE Trust for Edina with Patrick as trustee

Probate Court oversees the SAFE Trust for Edina

So Wilmer signed a will leaving one-half of his assets to a standard SAFE Trust for Patrick, and the other half to a Testamentary SAFE Trust for Edina. He named Patrick as trustee of Edina's Testamentary SAFE Trust, and Wilmer specified that Patrick was to use all of the trust income for Edina, as well as principal for anything she needed if the income was not sufficient. Wilmer rested much more comfortably knowing that the probate court would be watching over Patrick's shoulder, making sure that Edina's trust was being handled honestly and fairly. That peace of mind was extremely important for Wilmer, even though he realized there would be additional burdens and costs due to throwing the estate into probate.

Using a will combined with a Testamentary SAFE Trust will be the exception, rather than the rule. Usually you'll be better off avoiding probate. But if you feel you need the extra oversight offered by the probate court, then a will and Testamentary SAFE Trust may be the best way to go.

DON'T FORGET THE "LITTLE" ITEMS

We've been discussing how a Starter Trust combined with a SAFE Trust can allow you to leave your investments to your heirs, protecting them from probate, taxes, spouses, and lawsuits. The investments (e.g., home, bank accounts, CDs, stocks) are the big items. But it's the little items, those with the least economic value, that sometimes cause the biggest problems.

How should you leave your personal items like family photos, jewelry, china, artwork, silverware, home furnishings, and even the family Bible? Most people just leave everything equally to the kids. A simple statement in your trust, telling the kids to split your personal effects equally between them, is usually sufficient.

As a practical matter, the children typically come to an agreement as to who gets what, and everything works out fine—if not perfectly, at least well enough. For example, your son John may take the antique cabinet and Hummels because he's a collector, your daughter Bonnie gets your jewelry because she's the only daughter; each child gets back the items they gave to Mom as gifts over the years; they hold a garage sale for the rest of the furnishings that neither child desires; and they donate any unsold items to charity.

What if the heirs can't agree? That's when the problems come up. Let me tell you about two cases.

The Tale of Alice

A story of "biblical proportions" appeared in the news a couple of years ago. It involved a woman, Alice, who died in January 2000, leaving her estate equally to her two children. Unfortunately, like Cain and Abel, her children battled. The source of the discord was who should get the family Bible. After years of conflict, a probate judge finally settled their dispute using Solomonic wisdom: he ordered that the Bible should be auctioned and the proceeds split between the children. It was a practical solution, but the family heirloom, which had far more personal than financial value, was gone forever. So who really won?

The Story of Ivan and Marta

A wealthy gentleman died, leaving very nice inheritances to a variety of heirs. Two family members, Ivan and Marta, received apartment buildings, worth millions of dollars. But they were not satisfied, and took their grievances to court. Contrary to what you might think, they were not fighting over the valuable rental properties. No, they went to war over a picture of the old man. The painting itself had absolutely no financial value. To be honest, it wasn't great art. But both Ivan and Marta claimed they wanted the picture for sentimental reasons. The quest for the painting became a power struggle.

The lawyers proposed several compromise solutions, such as allowing the painting to go to one heir and giving other photos and memorabilia to the other. Ivan even offered Marta a tidy sum in exchange for the painting. But no agreement could be reached.

Although the multimillion-dollar apartment buildings were divided quickly and inexpensively, many months were spent viciously battling over that painting. The case was finally resolved when Ivan agreed to accept an expensive, high-quality reproduction of the painting. The estate was closed only after the two heirs had spent many thousands of dollars on litigation costs and destroyed their previously cordial relationship.

Are *your* heirs likely to battle after your death? Is there any way to set up your Starter Trust and SAFE Trust to preserve the peace when you're gone? Proper planning may help avoid warfare at your passing.

In the best of all possible worlds, family members are all highly rational individuals. But sadly, it seems death may cause some heirs to lose their mental faculties, resulting in some "heir-raising" stories! The courts are filled with family feuds triggered by wills and trusts that were not adequately specific when it came to the distribution of the personal effects.

Most wills and trusts give the executor or trustee broad discretion to divide the personal items so that each heir receives items that, in total, have a comparable market value. Or the executor or trustee may decide to sell everything and split the proceeds. But if the executor or trustee is one of the children, the other kids may end up with hard feelings.

Lots of folks leave a detailed note or list, in addition to the will or trust, describing who should get each item in the house. This approach may go a long way toward reducing fights between the kids. If they don't think the allocation of the personal items is fair, they can blame you. And guess what? You're gone!

The primary problem with a side note or list is that's it's not legally binding. While most heirs honor it, they don't have to.

If you want your list to be binding, in most states you'll have to put it into the Starter Trust, SAFE Trust, or will. But then every time you change your mind, you'll have to return to the lawyer to change the document.

Regardless of whether or not your list is in a trust or will, it should be as specific as possible. "My gold ring" may not be descriptive enough if you have more than one gold ring. Better wording would be: "My gold ring with the large center opal stone surrounded by five small diamonds."

You may try to avoid disputes after you're gone by giving things away during your life. The key problem here is that you must actually give the possessions to your kids; telling a child that the ring or TV is theirs but keeping it in your possession is not enough. And if you really give your personal possessions away, then you'll no longer be able to enjoy your possessions when they're in your children's homes. Are you prepared to see your grandchildren using "your" treasured antique loveseat as a trampoline?

There's no way to absolutely guarantee your heirs won't battle when you're gone. If they can't stand each other now, things won't miraculously get better after you've passed on. For some families, the best options might be to require that everything be sold at your death, or to give all your personal items to charity. Or just sell it all now, and spend the money—on yourself!

ENSURE THAT YOUR ESTATE GOES WHERE YOU INTENDED

When people go to the trouble and expense of creating Starter Trusts for themselves, while they're alive, with SAFE Trusts for their kids, troubles arising from assets winding up in the hands of the wrong people should be eliminated. But believe it or not, this unanticipated outcome actually still occurs.

How could this be possible? The answer is alarmingly simple. Failure to correctly specify the right beneficiary. Let me give you three examples.

First, let's say you want to leave money to your dear uncle, Robert Williams, either directly or into a SAFE Trust for him. So you establish a Starter Trust that distributes at your death into a SAFE Trust for Robert Williams. Yet when you die, your money never reaches your uncle. Instead, the SAFE Trust is held for his son, your cousin. What went wrong? It turns out your uncle's legal name is Robert J. Williams, Jr., and he goes by Bobby. His son is Robert J. Williams, III, and he goes by Robert.

Your cousin is now the happy recipient. Sure hope you like him!

Second, you expend a lot of time (and money) setting up elaborate SAFE Trusts, providing for the benefit of your three children. Unfortunately, at your death, your CDs and savings all pass to just one of your children, directly, and not into any SAFE Trust. What went wrong? You named the one child who lives near you as the joint owner of your accounts. Even though your Starter Trust says all the assets should go into SAFE Trusts for all three kids, the designation of a joint owner on the account itself takes precedence. Your one child gets the CDs and savings, with no SAFE protections, and the other kids are cut out completely. That outcome probably won't enhance sibling relations.

The third example involves organizations. Lots of folks who create SAFE Trusts for their kids or grandkids also designate a portion of their estate for their favorite charities. They may wish to help the church that aided them spiritually, or their college alma mater. The problem is that the inheritance often ends up elsewhere.

Here's a real case. A gentleman's wife died of complications from diabetes. They had received so much support from the local diabetes organization that this man wanted to say "thanks" by leaving the agency some money. So he named the diabetes association as beneficiary.

There was only one problem. There are at least three different diabetes groups that do business in Cleveland, where he lived. There's the Diabetes Association of Greater Cleveland; the American Diabetes Association, which has both a national and Cleveland presence; and the Juvenile Diabetes Foundation. All are completely independent. Since this kind gentleman failed to clearly specify which one, his money went to a good cause, but not the specific agency he had in mind.

Even if there's only one organization, your money still could end up in the wrong place. Let's say the Alzheimer's Association has provided comfort and care for your family. Naming the Alzheimer's Assocation as a beneficiary may not be enough. Without specifying that you want your money to go to the Cleveland Chapter, to help fund the work of the local support groups, your money instead may be sent to the national Alzheimer's Association office based in Chicago.

As you can see, if you are not as specific as possible, the outcome of your final wishes could be quite different from what you ever imagined! You can avoid problems by being precise and using exact names when listing beneficiaries, whether it be in your SAFE Trust, your will, or any other document.

HELP YOUR HEIRS FIND YOUR ASSETS

A client came in to my law office recently; there's nothing unusual about that. But you might think it's strange that she brought with her a plastic garbage bag stuffed to the brim. Without looking twice, I asked her to unload the contents on my conference room table!

This actually is not a rare event in my professional life. I'm a regular repository of mystery bags. Part of my job is to help the family uncover the secret financial life of the deceased. In this case, the client's mother had passed away, and her daughter had no clue what assets she had. The mother had always been a private person and never revealed her financial affairs to anyone. So now the daughter was forced to play Sherlock Holmes in order to try to figure out what her mom owned.

After her mom died, the daughter carefully went through her mother's home on a financial scavenger hunt. She was looking for bank and broker statements, insurance premium notices, tax forms, and anything else that might be a tip-off to her mom's assets. Then she brought in all these pieces of her mom's financial puzzle so that I could attempt to put together the big picture.

In this case, I think we uncovered everything. But it was a very time-consuming, frustrating process. And in many cases I'm sure that some assets are never found. The state governments become the lucky heirs by default, winding up with millions of dollars of assets that should have belonged to the families.

Just having a Starter Trust and a SAFE Trust doesn't solve the problem. As explained earlier in this chapter, while you're alive you must transfer (on paper) your assets into the name of the trustee of your trust. But assets in a trust are not necessarily all conveniently located in one place. You can have CDs and savings located at different banks, investments at a variety of brokerage houses, individually held stock certificates, a pile of savings bonds, your home, a couple of time shares, and so on. When you die, your child may have trouble locating your assets even if they're all titled in the name of your trust.

So what can you do to help your children or other heirs find all of your assets after your death? The best way is to talk with your heirs *now*, before you die. Tell them what you have and where it is.

But many folks want to keep their financial affairs private while they're alive. And that's understandable. Telling your children about what you own may invite your kids to stick their noses into your business, and to try to take control while you're still above ground. If you inform them that the assets are titled to a Revocable Living Trust that will pass the estate into SAFE Trusts, they may start asking the details—details you may not want to give them.

If you're not willing to talk about your assets with your kids, here's the next-best strategy.

Organize a catalogue of your assets in one place. Make a list of all your bank accounts, stocks, bonds, money markets, real estate, life insurance, annuities, and anything else you own. Attach copies of the account statements, stock certificates, insurance and annuity policies, and deeds to property. If you have a safe deposit box, keep the key with these papers as well.

Also keep your trust documents in the same place. And make a list of important people who may help your family when you're gone. Include the names and phone numbers of your accountant, doctor, financial adviser, and lawyer. Put this list and backup material in a file cabinet, or a box, or even in a kitchen cabinet. One client of mine put her "going away" materials in a suitcase, which she kept in the family room. A fireproof container might be best.

Whatever you put your papers in, label it clearly, so someone coming into the home will know what it is. And consider leaving copies with your lawyer.

Then talk to your alternate trustee, the person you'd like to handle things when you become incapacitated or die. Tell him that you've created a "going away" file and where it is. You don't have to reveal anything specific about your finances. But at least tell him that you've created a list and a trust, and where they can be found. (Then remember not to move them without informing your alternate trustee of the change!)

If you keep financial information on your computer, you'll also have to tell your alternate trustee where to look on your computer and give him your passwords. And if you use a safe deposit box at the bank to hold your asset list and legal documents, make sure your alternate trustee knows where to find the key.

Now, if you are the *child* reading this, talk to your parents. Ask them about their finances. Assure them that you are not just being nosy, but you are trying to help *them* achieve *their* goals. If that fails, show them this book and suggest they read it!

If despite your best efforts your parents still refuse to discuss their resources, or if you don't feel right asking, then at least suggest that your parents organize their finances and make a list. This is something loving parents should do for their children. The heirs will have plenty to do without having to devote months of their lives playing Sherlock Holmes to handle a parent's trust at death. Detective mysteries are great, as long as they're works of fiction.

UPDATE YOUR SAFE ESTATE PLAN

What if you make your Starter Trust and your SAFE Trusts for the children, and then you change your mind about who should get what or when they should get it? Can you change your plan? The short answer is yes.

Many of the Starter Trusts we've discussed are changeable, and even fully revocable, at any time you choose. The only Starter Trusts we've discussed that you cannot change, ever, are the Medicaid Trust, the Creditor Protection Trust, and the Life Insurance Trust. These three Starter Trusts are irrevocable and nonchangeable.

Most SAFE Trusts are also revocable and changeable while you're alive and competent. The only one that you can't fiddle with is the Crummey SAFE Trust.

Only two requirements must be met: you must be competent and alive. Demonstrating that you are "still kicking" is a pretty straightforward test. Proving competence is sometimes less so. We'll address the tests for competence later in this chapter.

Assuming you're competent and alive, and the Starter Trust is one that's changeable, you may amend it at any time. An amendment must be done formally, by signing a separate document. If the change is simple, perhaps just changing the name of an alternate trustee, the amendment document can be simple. But *don't* just cross out something on your trust and write in the change—not only won't that work, you could invalidate the entire trust.

Both a Starter and a SAFE Trust are complicated documents. They are not something you can do yourself. And an amendment is no different. You'll need a lawyer to prepare it for you. The fees for small changes shouldn't be astronomical, so don't let that concern jeopardize the validity of the trust.

You should review your Starter and SAFE Trust yourself at least once a year, to make sure it still does what you wish. Maybe you've named your child as trustee of his SAFE Trust, but your child has become extremely ill and can no longer manage his finances. Or perhaps you've named a grandchild as a beneficiary of a SAFE Trust, and you don't speak to that grandchild any longer. These are just some of the reasons that might cause you to consider amending your SAFE Trust.

A variety of events may trigger the need for a change. These include:

- *Your child gets married.* This is the primary reason people decide to create or change SAFE Trusts. You might not have felt you needed a

SAFE Trust while your child was single, or maybe you set it up in a way that now makes less sense. For example, you may have named your son as trustee of his own SAFE Trust and as an alternate trustee for your daughter's SAFE Trust. Now that you've met your son's wife, and you see how controlling she is of your son, you'd rather remove him from serving both as trustee for his SAFE Trust and as a backup trustee for your daughter's SAFE Trust.

- *Your child gets a divorce.* This also is one of the main reasons that people decide to create or change a SAFE Trust. Why? Because many people don't believe their children will ever divorce until one child actually does. In addition, a child's divorce creates the potential for a future remarriage. The inheritance you are leaving a child may wind up with your child's new spouse whom you don't even know.

- *A beneficiary or trustee dies.* A death of a family member or friend sometimes requires changing your SAFE Trust, sometimes not. A well-written SAFE Trust will have several alternatives at every position. Let's say you name your son Joe as trustee of his SAFE Trust, followed by your brother Tim. If Tim dies, you may wish to add another alternative.

- *You get rid of or acquire assets.* Let's say you originally left your Merrill Lynch brokerage account to your son Bob's SAFE Trust, but now you've switched to A. G. Edwards. If you still want Bob to receive the account on your death, an update is in order. (It's usually best not to leave specific accounts to specific people; better is just to place all the assets into the Starter Trust, then leave a percentage or amount to each SAFE Trust).

- *Your assets change in value.* You want to divide your assets equally among your children's SAFE Trusts. But because some asset values have increased or decreased, the specified gifts are no longer equal. For example, perhaps you own the house in which your daughter is living, and you want the home to go into her SAFE Trust at your death. At the time you set up the trust, that home was worth $100,000. Attempting to be fair to all, you left $100,000 to each of your two sons' SAFE Trusts, and then provided that everything else would be split equally into the three SAFE Trusts for your three kids. But now the house for your daughter is worth $200,000. You may need to adjust the "catch-up" amounts for the other two children's SAFE Trusts. (Or you may be better off requiring that the house must be appraised at your death and that the other two children will be given an equal amount into their SAFE Trusts based on that appraisal; that way you won't have to constantly amend your trust.)

- *You change your mind about when an heir should inherit.* Let's say you specified that if your child dies with assets still in his SAFE Trust, your grandchildren would receive the remaining assets outright, but only after reaching the age of eighteen. Now that your grandchildren have reached eighteen, but still act as if they're ten, you've decided that it would be more prudent to safeguard the inheritance for them until they're more mature, perhaps age thirty. You'll have to revise the SAFE Trust.

- *The status of a beneficiary changes.* The personal circumstances of one of your beneficiaries has changed significantly in some way (perhaps he lost a job, or won the lottery) and you wish to increase or decrease the share going into that child's SAFE Trust.

- *Changed circumstances of a trustee.* Let's say you originally named your brother as an alternate trustee for a child's SAFE Trust. While that may have been a good selection at the time, your brother himself has become ill and can no longer serve. Of course, that may require a change to the SAFE Trust.

- *Your worth increases dramatically.* You receive an inheritance or other windfall that alters your estate tax considerations. Wouldn't that be a nice problem to have? After you finish celebrating, you'll want to review your Starter and SAFE Trust to maximize potential tax savings. For example, you might want to create an A-B Starter Trust, a Death Tax Protection SAFE Trust, and/or a Dynasty SAFE Trust (see Chapters 3 and 4).

In addition to reviewing the Starter and SAFE Trust yourself annually, you should also have it reviewed by a lawyer every three or four years. An experienced lawyer should advise you whether changes are needed due to changes in the law. For example, the federal death tax rules may change, requiring a modification; your state may adopt or change its own estate taxes, requiring a change in your trust; the Medicaid rules seem to be constantly in flux, and a change in the law may require a modification to your documents.

BULLETPROOF YOUR PLANS AGAINST CHALLENGES

When your son married, you looked forward to having an expanded family. Unfortunately, things haven't turned out the way you hoped. Your daughter-in-law is a miserable person. It's clear that she gets great joy out of making your life unpleasant. But what's even worse is that she's money-hungry and has turned your son against you. Although you do it with a heavy heart, you've decided to cut your son out of your trust entirely. The problem is, if you do, you're sure your daughter-in-law will cause trouble after you die. She'll probably file a lawsuit to contest your trust.

Or maybe you gave your son some money to start a business, or to buy a home, and so you'd like to leave your daughter a larger inheritance. But since your son doesn't think your earlier largesse should count against him, he may challenge the plan.

Does this sound familiar? Would you like to cut a family member out of any inheritance, or at least leave one relative a smaller share of your estate? Is there any way to protect against challenges?

There's no way to prevent your child, in-law, or anyone else from filing a lawsuit to try to overturn your trust after you're gone. But the important question is: Can they win? And the good news is that there are a number of steps you can take to protect both your Starter Trust and your SAFE Trusts from successfully being overturned.

To overturn your trust, a challenger must prove at least one of the following:

- The trust did not follow the legal requirements for making a valid trust. For example, the trust may not have the proper number of witnesses, or the witnesses may have been related to you in violation of state law.

- You were not mentally competent to make the trust (discussed below).

- Someone exerted "undue influence" over you, overpowering your own independent judgment and causing you to dispose of your money and property contrary to your real wishes and desires. For example, if the reason you left everything to your son was that he held a gun to your head, then you've been subject to undue influence, and the trust can be thrown out. In reality, undue influence is typically much more subtle. Perhaps your daughter said she would stop making your meals, taking you to the doctor, and cleaning your house, and threatened to put you into a nursing home, if you didn't leave her the bulk of your estate. That's undue influence if the threat overcomes your free will. But if your daughter just asks for more of the estate because she's doing more for you, and you agree, that alone probably is not undue influence.

- Someone committed fraud, leading you into making the trust by misrepresentation or deception. Perhaps your son told you that the document you were signing was a trust leaving your estate for all three of your kids, when it really only benefitted him, and he wouldn't let you read the relevant pages. Or perhaps he substituted retyped pages giving him everything after you signed the trust with a different distribution plan. That's fraud.

  If your daughter made up nasty stories about your son in order to get you to cut your son out of the trust, and it works, your son may be able to have the trust set aside on the basis of fraud.

  But let's change the example slightly. You heard a story about your son and changed your trust to leave everything to your daughter as a result. The story was wrong, and you made a mistake. But there was no fraud or undue influence by your daughter—she had nothing to do with it. In that case, the trust remains as is; the mistake is not sufficient for a court to invalidate the trust.

For a mistake to invalidate your trust, you generally will have to have been mistaken about the nature of the document signed—not understanding that you signed a trust. That situation obviously arises only rarely.

What if the lawyer who writes up the trust makes a mistake? You tell the lawyer you wish to leave your house to your daughter, but the lawyer misunderstands and leaves it to your son. If something is written into the trust by mistake, and you don't realize that when you sign, the trust probably is invalid, although state laws vary. To avoid any problems, you should make sure you understand what the trust says before you sign, even if it means asking the lawyer to take the time to review it with you line by line and word by word.

Competence, or more accurately incompetence, is the most common basis for attacking trusts, along with wills and other legal documents. In order to make a valid trust that can withstand a legal challenge, you must have "sound mind and memory." But what does that really mean?

For a person to be considered to have "sound mind and memory," four tests must be satisfied. At the time a person makes a trust, he (or she) must be able to:

- Understand what it is he is doing (e.g., making a trust leaving money and property to heirs)
- Comprehend the nature and extent (amount) of his money and property
- Understand who his closest family members are and his relationships to them
- Make a rational judgment about how to leave his money and property at death

Not every impairment of mind or memory will disqualify a person from making a trust. You do not have to be mentally sound in all ways and at all times.

For example, you may have the capacity to make a trust even if you are sometimes forgetful or at times unable to recognize your children. Memory loss from Alzheimer's, dementia, or other causes comes in varying degrees and qualities. If you are able to recall the property you wish to dispose of by your trust, to understand how you wish to distribute it, and to comprehend who you wish to make your heirs, you may be able to make a trust despite weakness of mind or memory.

Let's say you are in the hospital being given various drugs. Can you make a valid trust?

As I have already explained, when it comes to determining a person's capacity, there are rarely black-and-white answers. Just because a person is taking drugs does not automatically preclude that person from making a trust. The question is: At the time you make the trust, is your mental state so altered by the drugs that you are unable to satisfy the tests listed above?

The same principles apply to other potential impairments. If a person is of advanced years, has failing eyesight or hearing, changes subjects frequently in a discussion and doesn't focus well, or has trouble communicating, that does not mean he does not have adequate capacity to make a trust. Your trust can be valid as long as you understand what you are doing at the time you make the trust.

Courts have even ruled that a person who has been placed under a guardianship or declared insane may still have the capacity to make legal documents. For example, a person may be incompetent one moment, lucid another. As long as a trust is made during a lucid period, it may be valid.

Now that we've explained under what circumstances your trust may be successfully challenged, let's talk about the steps you can take to bulletproof your estate distribution plan from attack.

Bulletproofer 1: Use a Trust, Not a Will

Just using a Starter Trust and SAFE Trusts offers better protection against lawsuits than a will. The legal standards for overturning a will or trust are basically the same. But from a practical standpoint, a trust is stronger because it's private. When you use a will to pass assets at death, the will, along with an accounting of your entire estate, must be filed in probate court. Your disgruntled relatives will know exactly how and what you left to each member of the family (see Chapter 1). But with trusts, it's much harder (not impossible, but harder) for a family member to find out what you did. And that veil of secrecy helps protect your estate from lawsuits.

Bulletproofer 2: Get a Letter from the Doctor

As mentioned above, the most common basis for challenging a trust is that the person making it wasn't competent, didn't understand what she was doing. Just before finalizing your trust, get a letter from the doctor stating that you are competent and capable of making a trust.

Ask the doctor to be as specific and detailed as possible. The more information the doctor provides, the better. That is, unless the doctor does not believe that you are competent enough to make a trust.

There's a risk when you ask a doctor to write a letter. He might write a bad one, or refuse to write any letter, because he doesn't believe you to be competent. If you get a bad letter, or the doctor refuses to write any letter, that fact may be discovered during a future lawsuit contesting your trust, and it will provide significant evidence *against* the validity of the trust.

Bulletproofer 3: Talk with the Witnesses

In many states, the law requires that your trust have at least two or three witnesses who are not related to you. In most cases, the witnesses are there primarily to confirm that you actually signed the document.

But you may wish to explain your plan to the witnesses, describing why you are treating one relative less favorably than others. Then if your estate plan is later challenged, the witnesses to your trust may be able to support your competence.

Your lawyer may also be a key witness if there is ever a contest. No lawyer should ever allow a client to sign a trust without first talking to the client and ascertaining the client's competence. The lawyer should keep good notes so that he can testify to your competence and free will, if that's ever needed.

Bulletproofer 4: Make a Videotape

Create proof that you knew what you were doing, you were competent, and you were under no undue pressure from another family member when you signed your trust. Make a videotape stating your reasons for cutting out your son, or for leaving a larger inheritance to your daughter. Have your lawyer pose questions to you on tape. Don't allow other family members to watch, so that no one can claim that others intimidated or influenced you. A videotape may provide wonderful protection against lawsuits.

But again, a videotape can also work against the validity of your trust. If you get flustered and forget things, stumble over words, make mistakes, and generally sound confused, a challenger to your trust will use that tape to argue that the trust should be thrown out. And you can't just "cut out the bad parts" or edit the tape. The challenger will be entitled to know whether a tape was made, and whether it was thrown out or edited. If a tape was made and destroyed, or edited, a judge or jury may assume the worst.

Bulletproofer 5: Add an "In Terrorem" Clause

Most states allow a practical way to discourage lawsuits: you may provide in your trust that anyone who contests the trust loses his or her inheritance. So let's say you leave your son Bill $10,000. While that's less than the other kids will receive, Bill gets *nothing* if he challenges the trust. With this "in terrorem" or "no contest" clause, Bill will think long and hard before starting trouble.

When you use an "in terrorem" clause, you'll also have to leave the likely contestant enough money to make him concerned about losing. Leaving him $10 will never be enough. Leaving him $10,000 out of a $200,000 estate may be sufficient. But leaving $10,000 from a $2 million trust, from which he'd get $650,000 if he won the challenge, is probably not enough to cause him to abandon his lawsuit.

So you can bulletproof your estate from lawsuits by making a trust, getting a letter from a doctor, explaining your intentions to witnesses, making a videotape, and/or adding an "in terrorem" clause. If you want to cut out your son and daughter-in-law, do it. Don't be afraid of a legal challenge; in reality, challenges occur relatively infrequently. If you're concerned that your heirs might get angry with you, forget about it. It's your money and you have every right to distribute it as you see fit. Besides, you won't be around to hear their grumbling!

CHAPTER 8

The Documents
You Need

As you should see by now, Starter Trusts and SAFE Trusts are very important documents that can achieve many important financial and personal goals for you and your family. But even a Starter Trust/SAFE Trust combination is not itself enough for a comprehensive plan. I know it sounds as if you will be buried in paper, but you must have additional legal documents to accompany and coordinate with the trusts to ensure that you and your family are fully protected. These are a Pourover Will, a Financial Durable Power of Attorney, a Health Care Durable Power of Attorney, and a Living Will.

POUROVER WILL

I've explained how the most common and protective SAFE plans will almost always combine a Starter Trust for you with SAFE Trusts for the kids. The Revocable Living Trust is the simplest and most used Starter Trust; it will protect you during your lifetime, providing management in case you become incapacitated, and then pass your assets to SAFE Trusts for your heirs at your death with no probate. You might be wondering, then, if the Revocable Living Trust takes care of your estate when you die, avoiding probate, do you still need to make a will (even though a will passes assets *through* probate)? The answer is yes. Everyone should have a will, even if you have a trust. Don't worry, this won't force you into probate. You'll see the role of the will is slightly different when you have a trust. I'll explain how the pieces of this estate planning puzzle fit together.

Let's start with a Revocable Living Trust. Picture it like a basket. You fill it with your assets while you're alive by changing the names on your accounts to the name of the trust. Instead of having your name, Mary Smith, on your bank account, stocks, and real estate, you change the titles to Mary Smith, Trustee of the Mary Smith Trust dated (the date the trust was signed). In Chapter 7, we discussed how to fund your trust. At your death, all the assets in your trust "basket" pass to the SAFE Trusts for your heirs. Even if you have a will, your trust controls where your assets in the trust go at death. If *all* your assets are in your Revocable Living Trust at your death, the problem is avoided and the will is moot—it won't do anything. So why make a will if you have a funded trust?

Two reasons.

First, because you are a fallible human being, you may forget to put something into the Starter Trust during your lifetime. Lots of people forget to put cars into the trust, for example. Or maybe you didn't even recall that you had some old savings bonds, and those never made it into the trust. A trust only covers things that you've remembered to put into it during your lifetime. Your will serves as an important backup. It will cover assets that you forgot to put into the Revocable Living Trust.

The will to accompany a trust is called a Pourover Will. It's not the same as the standard will you'd make *without* a trust. A Pourover Will is coordinated with your trust, and would very simply state that any assets passing under the will shall go into, shall "pour" into, your trust at death. The trust is your main document; *it* states where your assets go and funnels your estate into the SAFE Trusts for your kids. The Pourover Will is very simple, and makes sure that any assets that may have inadvertently been omitted from your Starter Trust will get there after you're gone. It's the safety net for your estate.

The second reason to make a Pourover Will is to name an executor (also called a personal representative) to handle any lawsuits that might arise at your death.

Let's say that you die as a result of an auto accident. Some drunk driver runs a stoplight and sends you prematurely to the life beyond. Or perhaps your death results from a case of medical negligence. Your spouse or children may decide that justice should be done and a lawsuit should be filed on your behalf, on behalf of the estate.

Your surviving relatives won't automatically be permitted to sue for you or the estate. Children, even a spouse, cannot just step in to represent the estate's interests. And a trustee (or alternate trustee) of a trust generally isn't permitted to handle a lawsuit for the estate either. The only person with the legal right to sue for the estate and represent your interests is the executor named under your will.

If you don't have a will, one of your family members may go to the probate court and ask that a representative be appointed to administer your estate and handle the lawsuit. But the probate judge has the power to select the representative, and there's no guarantee that the probate judge will appoint the person you would have picked. And it's always more complicated and expensive to process an estate and lawsuit with no will than when a will was prepared.

Also keep in mind that if a lawsuit must be pursued, and it is successful, there will be money paid to the estate. That money could not have been put into your Revocable Living Trust during your lifetime, because you didn't have the money then. So you'll need a Pourover Will to make sure any money recovered in a lawsuit will pass into the trust and gain the valuable SAFE protections for your heirs.

FINANCIAL DURABLE POWER OF ATTORNEY

Let's say you are seriously injured in a car accident, or you suffer a stroke, or you are stricken with Alzheimer's disease, and you can no longer handle your financial affairs. Your spouse, child, or other loved ones cannot automatically step in to pay your bills and help with your affairs just because they're related to you. They can't take money from your IRA or 401(k), even to pay *your* bills. Only *you* can make withdrawals from these accounts, and only if you are competent to do so.

Your loved ones can't sell or refinance the home just because they're your relatives. If you or your spouse is named on the house deed, you would have to sign to sell or refinance the home. And you could only do so if competent.

Unfortunately, financial disasters like this are played out every day. When a person becomes incompetent, unable to handle his affairs, no one has an automatic right to step in to help. The money gets stuck in the hands of the incapacitated person and can't be used. Without proper planning, the only solution would be a guardianship. A loved one may go to court—that's the dreaded Probate Court—and ask that a guardian be appointed. A guardian (sometimes known as a "conservator," "curator," "committee," "tutor," or "fiduciary") may be appointed, with the oversight and permission of the probate judge, to manage the finances of the person who's incapacitated.

A guardianship works, but it involves costs, paperwork, and hassles. It's really very similar to the probate process at death—with one major difference. Probate at death may take a year or two. Probate of a guardianship will last as long as the individual remains incapacitated, because the probate judge must watch over the incapacited person for as long as that person is alive and unable to handle his/her own affairs. If you fear the costs and frustrations of a one-year probate process at death, imagine a twenty-year probate of a guardianship!

A funded Revocable Living Trust (or some other Starter Trust) goes a long way to avoiding the need for a guardianship, and provides many valuable protections when a person becomes incapacitated. I've already discussed how you would name backup trustees, so if you become incapacitated and unable to handle your affairs, there's someone who you trust already lined up to step in and take over.

So if you have a Revocable Living Trust with alternate trustees, do you need a Financial Durable Power of Attorney? The answer is: absolutely.

There's a limit to a Revocable Living Trust and other Starter Trusts. Your alternate trustee can handle and manage only your assets that are in the trust. And some assets *cannot* be put into the trust, including IRAs, 401(k)s, and other tax-deferred retirement accounts. To provide management for these assets, you must have a Financial Durable Power of Attorney. And your legal affairs can only be handled under a Financial Durable Power of Attorney.

A Financial Durable Power of Attorney (DPA) is a relatively simple legal document that authorizes someone you trust—usually a spouse or child—to manage your assets that are *not* in the trust. This is your "agent" or "attorney-in-fact." The maker is often called the "principal." Probably the most significant assets that will not be in your trust will be your tax-deferred investments: IRAs, 401(k)s, 403(b)s, and annuities. As I explained in Chapter 7, these retirement assets cannot be put into a trust without losing the tax-deferred status and incurring an immediate tax (annuities may be an exception to this rule, but the law is not yet settled). The trustee of your trust will not be able to touch your tax-deferred investments outside of the trust, but your agent named in the Financial Durable Power of Attorney can.

The Financial Durable Power of Attorney goes well beyond authorizing an agent to manage your retirement accounts. It allows your agent to handle any legal issues that come up.

For example, let's say a contract must be signed admitting you to a nursing home or assisted-living facility, or to hire home health care aides. But you're not competent to execute the necessary paperwork. The trustee of your trust cannot help you, but your agent under the Financial Durable Power of Attorney can. Or maybe it's necessary to take out a loan to pay some of your bills, or your auto lease is coming due and it's advisable to buy the car. You can't sign the necessary papers if you're not competent, and the trustee of your trust can't help, but your agent under the Financial Durable Power of Attorney has the power to handle your legal affairs.

Note that there's a difference between a "regular" and a "durable" financial power of attorney.

A *regular* power of attorney can *only* be used while you are *competent* and capable of handling your own affairs. It might be used, for example, to authorize someone to handle your finances while you're out of the country on business. It becomes ineffective and stops working the moment the maker (you) becomes incompetent.

A *Durable* Financial Power of Attorney remains valid even after the maker becomes incompetent. Since the time an individual is most likely to need a power of attorney is when he or she becomes incompetent, this is no small difference. An adult should have a *Durable* Financial Power of Attorney for his or her protection.

The language difference between a regular and Durable Financial Power of Attorney is usually only a sentence or two. A Durable Financial Power of Attorney will include language stating that the document remains valid and effective even if the person making it becomes incompetent or otherwise unable to handle his or her own affairs.

The Financial Durable Power of Attorney should be coordinated with your trust, giving the agent under the DPA and the trustee of your trust the power to work together without any conflicts of interest. You may name the same person who serves as the alternate trustee (to you) under the trust to serve as the agent under the Financial Durable Power of Attorney, or you may decide to name two different people.

The Financial Durable Power of Attorney is a powerful document. It authorizes someone else to take money from your retirement accounts and any other accounts not in a trust. As you can imagine, that creates a great deal of risk. Legally, the person to whom you give a Financial Durable Power of Attorney can act only in your best interest. He can take money from your IRA, but only if he uses it *for you*. He can't legally raid your account and take the money for a trip to Paris for himself. But as a practical matter, if someone does abuse your trust and misuses the DPA, you will have a legal nightmare.

Picking a trustworthy agent is the best way to limit the risk. Normally this means selecting your spouse, your child, or a close friend.

The person to whom you give your Financial Durable Power of Attorney does not, under the laws of most states, have to live in the same state. But for convenience and speed of action, it is preferable to choose someone who lives reasonably close by.

Although the person you select is called an "attorney-in-fact," he or she does not have to be a lawyer; the attorney-in-fact also need not be a financial planner, businessperson, or accountant, or in any other particular profession. Sure, it's helpful if the recipient of a Financial Durable Power of Attorney has some understanding of finances and the legal impact of a Financial Durable Power of Attorney, but it's not required. The most important consideration is that you trust the person to whom you are entrusting your Financial Durable Power of Attorney.

Because the Financial Durable Power of Attorney is such a powerful document, you'll want to take precautions to protect yourself against financial abuse. Here are four other techniques you can use to help prevent unauthorized use of your assets.

1. *You may create a "Springing" Financial Durable Power of Attorney.* With this type of DPA, the document can only be used after at least one doctor has written a note stating that you are no longer capable of handling your own finances. It "springs" into effect at that time. This is similar to the requirement that must be satisfied before your alternate trustee of your Revocable Living Trust can take over for you.

   "Springing" Financial Durable Powers of Attorney have not yet been accepted in all states, and even where they are used, they often invite legal challenges over the issue of defining the actual onset of incapacity.

   In addition, getting a doctor's note may not be easy, especially if you become irrational and paranoid and refuse to see a physician. Without the doctor's certification, the Springing Financial Durable Power of Attorney is useless. If your Financial DPA is *not* springing, it may be used by the agent immediately, without the need for a doctor's certification. Obviously, this ability to use the Financial Durable Power of Attorney at *any* time could pose problems if you don't have a trustworthy agent.

2. *You may name two or more coagents who must act together.* For example, you may provide that all three of your children are coagents and must sign the paperwork necessary to withdraw funds from your IRA accounts. That way, your kids may steal from you only if they all work together! But naming coagents who must act together can be burdensome, requiring them to get together, sign paperwork together, and agree—not always easy. And naming multiple agents can create delays.

3. *You may name one child as the agent under the Financial DPA but actually give physical control of the document to a second child.* Again, the document cannot be used, or abused, unless both children cooperate. The person holding the Financial Durable Power of Attorney can't use it because he's not named in it, and your named agent can't use it unless the person holding it gives the document to him.

4. *You may name one person as agent but have your attorney hold the Financial DPA until the time that it's truly needed.* You may even instruct the attorney to give it to the agent *only* when the attorney determines it should be used for your benefit. Of course, for this to work, you must trust your attorney. Come on, now—no lawyer jokes, please!

While none of these four protections is perfect, each one makes it difficult for the power of a Financial DPA to be abused. Make your choice based on what you think will work best for you.

Now that I've covered the basics of the Financial Durable Power of Attorney, let's answer three of the most common questions people ask.

CAN I GIVE A SEPARATE FINANCIAL DURABLE POWER OF ATTORNEY TO MORE THAN ONE PERSON?

You can name as many individuals as you like as agents and give them each a Financial Durable Power of Attorney. You could give one to each of your three kids, one to Aunt Macey, and one to your lawyer. But I don't advise it.

As I've said, these are powerful documents. If it's risky giving a Financial Durable Power of Attorney to *one* person, it's more risky to give two or three people Financial Durable Powers of Attorney. Each person you give one to has full powers to act for you.

There are very few occasions when I'd recommend giving out more than one Financial Durable Power of Attorney. In the case of elderly parents, each may want to give one Financial Durable Power of Attorney to the other, and another Financial Durable Power of Attorney to a child (so that there will be a greater likelihood that at least the child will be able to help out). If you have two children and don't want to show favoritism, you may want to give each child a Financial Durable Power of Attorney. Still, you are best off minimizing the number of Financial Durable Powers of Attorney that you hand around.

CAN I CANCEL A FINANCIAL DURABLE POWER OF ATTORNEY?

In most states, you can easily cancel a Financial Durable Power of Attorney. In theory all you need to do is declare that it's canceled. You usually aren't even required to put the cancellation in writing; just announce it to the holder, preferably in the presence of witnesses. That's in theory; now let's talk reality. Effectively canceling a Financial Durable Power of Attorney may be much harder.

Let's say that you announce to your friend that a Financial Durable Power of Attorney you granted to her is canceled. Your friend immediately goes to the bank with her Financial Durable Power of Attorney and tries to take out your IRA. The bank personnel won't know that you have canceled the Financial Durable Power of Attorney; they'll see a document that looks valid, and your friend (some friend!) can take the money and run.

In practice, you would have to try to get back all copies of the Financial Durable Power of Attorney. But that's not easy, since the friend could have made any number of copies, and many financial institutions will accept photocopies.

Of course, you could also give notice of the cancellation, in writing, not only to the agent but also to all those people and institutions (like your bank) you believe might be asked to honor the Financial Durable Power of Attorney. But it's usually impossible to predict everyone who may be asked to take some action based on a Financial Durable Power of Attorney.

If worse comes to worst, you could go to court and have a judge order that all copies be returned. But that's a hassle and expense you don't need. Better to minimize the risk in the first place by giving a Financial Durable Power of Attorney only to someone whom you trust.

CAN I PREPARE MY OWN
FINANCIAL DURABLE POWER OF ATTORNEY?

A Financial Durable Power of Attorney does not have to be complicated, but I generally wouldn't recommend preparing your own. Here are the basic elements that a Financial Durable Power of Attorney must include: it must be in writing, signed by the principal, and it must state the name of the person who is being authorized to act for the principal and the scope of his or her powers.

Every state has its own rules governing the use of a Financial Durable Power of Attorney. Because laws differ significantly concerning the use, execution, and recording of Financial Durable Powers of Attorney, and because the laws change frequently, it is always good procedure to consult a lawyer. Since Financial Durable Powers of Attorney are relatively simple to prepare, you shouldn't have to pay any more than about $250 for a lawyer to make one for you.

HEALTH CARE DURABLE POWER OF ATTORNEY

Generally speaking, a power of attorney authorizes another person to make decisions and/or act for you, the maker; many people have used powers of attorney at some time or another.

We've just talked about the importance of making a Financial Durable Power of Attorney, to coordinate with your Starter Trust. There's a closely related document, called a Health Care Durable Power of Attorney, that's equally important.

Let's say a doctor would like to try a procedure to diagnose your illness. Or perhaps he is suggesting amputating your foot to save your life. If you are conscious and competent, you can make your own decision. But what if you're unconscious, or otherwise unable to make your own health decisions?

Doctors can't just do things to you without permission (except in certain emergencies). In the past, doctors would tend to patients after "informal" discussions with the family. But the rash of lawsuits has put a stop to informal decision-making.

Lots of folks *mistakenly* think that their spouse or loving child will be permitted to step in and make health care decisions for them. Sadly, that's just not true. Your spouse, child, or other family member will *only* be allowed to make your health care decisions if you give them the authority to do so—and that's where the Health Care Durable Power of Attorney comes in.

Most states now allow you to appoint an agent (or "surrogate" or "proxy")—usually a trusted relative or friend—to make decisions about your medical care. The document is effective *only* if and when you cannot make your own health care decisions.

A Health Care DPA permits your agent to make a wide range of health care decisions: decisions involving medications, therapy, and even surgery. These decisions range from lifesaving to life termination.

A trustee under your Revocable Living Trust generally has no authority to make health care decisions for you. A Health Care Durable Power of Attorney is a necessary accompaniment to your trust.

LIVING WILL

On January 11, 1983, a young woman named Nancy Cruzan lost control of her car as she traveled down Elm Road in Jasper County, Missouri. The vehicle overturned, and Nancy was found lying in a ditch, unconscious. The paramedics were able to restore her breathing and heartbeat, but tragically not soon enough to prevent permanent brain damage from the oxygen deprivation she experienced.

Nancy's parents naturally held out hope for a recovery. To sustain her, feeding and water tubes were inserted. Nancy resided in a Missouri state hospital for years in a "persistent vegetative state". Although her eyes might open, Nancy's brain no longer processed information.

After it became apparent that Nancy had virtually no chance of recovery, that she would never regain an awareness of her surroundings, her parents asked the hospital to "pull the plug"—to terminate the artificial life supports and allow her to pass on. But the hospital refused, which triggered a long, emotionally draining court battle ending in the U.S. Supreme Court.

In a landmark decision, the Supreme Court ruled that each American has a Constitutional right "to determine what shall be done with his own body," and that includes the right to refuse unwanted medical treatment.

Since Nancy was clearly unable to speak for herself, the State of Missouri required "clear and convincing evidence" of her wishes. The evidence presented at the initial trial primarily consisted of Nancy's statements made to a housemate about a year before the accident stating that she would not want to live life as a "vegetable." The U.S. Supreme Court upheld the Missouri Court's decision that these statements were not sufficient proof of Nancy's desire to have hydration and nutrition withdrawn. Only after the presentation of more evidence of Nancy's wishes was Nancy taken off the life supports.

A second true situation involved Sally White (her name has been changed since her case never went to court). In April 2001, Sally was driving to her home near Alliance, Ohio. She too lost control of her car and it flipped over. Sally, unconscious, was life-flighted to Akron General Hospital, where she was hooked up to a respirator and a feeding tube to keep her alive.

Sally was in a "persistent vegetative state"—she was entirely unresponsive. After a few days of trying to revive her, the doctors concluded there was no hope. Since she was only thirty-five years old, her heart was strong, and the machines could keep her body alive. But she would never come out of her comalike state.

Sally had a very close, loving family. Her father, her three siblings, and her sixteen-year-old daughter held vigil at the hospital. (Her mother had passed away.) After the doctors issued their pronouncement, the family made the hardest decision any family could ever make—they agreed to ask the doctors to cease their heroic measures and allow Sally to pass away peacefully.

Sally had verbally told members of her family that she would not want to be hooked to life-support machines. But being young, she probably figured there was no hurry to put her thoughts down in writing. Fortunately, Sally's family was in complete agreement, and the doctors acceded to their wishes.

But Sally's scenario is more often the exception than the rule. Families often don't agree. And even when they do, doctors frequently are unwilling to "pull the plug" without specific authorization for fear of lawsuits.

The outcome of Sally's story certainly contrasts with Terri Schiavo's case, which played out in Florida. After suffering brain damage in connection with a heart attack in 1990, Terri reportedly lapsed into a "persistent vegetative state." Terri's husband, Michael, contended that she told him she'd never want to live that way. Michael wanted the feeding tube removed, and a court agreed. But Terri's parents fought Michael, and Governor Bush, along with the Florida legislature, stepped in to require that Terri's feeding tube be reinserted. Following years of litigation, the Florida Supreme Court ruled that Terri should be allowed to die, and the U.S. Supreme Court declined to accept a further appeal. After a fierce legal battle, Terri was permitted to die.

While these three cases all involved younger people, most of the cases involving life-and-death decisions concern older folks. If your mom or dad suffered a devastating stroke, do you know their wishes? And if your brain shut down, would your spouse or children understand how you would like them to proceed?

What's the lesson to be drawn from these heart-wrenching stories? Think about your values—how would *you* want to be treated if you could not speak for yourself? Then don't wait; express your wishes *clearly* to friends and family, and put those wishes in writing. The Supreme Court has said you have the right to make these decisions, but a court can't help you if your wishes remain unstated or unclear.

Now, you might be wondering how to go about putting your wishes on paper. A Living Will is a legal document that tells your family, doctors, and friends what medical treatments you would like, and would not like, at the end of your life. You should specify your wishes regarding artificial or mechanical life supports, including artificially supplied nutrition and hydration (feeding and water tubes). Make a Living Will now, while you can, but don't worry—it only becomes effective in the event that you cannot make your own decisions.

Don't be confused. A Living Will is not the same as a will or a living trust. Your will deals with the distribution of money or property at death; a living trust can be used to hold and manage money and property during your lifetime or after death. Neither addresses the issue of withholding or terminating medical treatment.

You should prepare a Living Will now, while you are still of sound mind and capable of communicating. If you are later diagnosed with a terminal illness, another Living Will should be prepared. The purpose of this is to avoid challenges to the first Living Will's validity. No one can then say that it was executed while you were healthy and that your feelings may have changed after becoming ill.

Once the Living Will is signed, copies should be given to family, doctors, clergy, and very close friends. The document should also be posted at home, where an EMS team could easily see it. Carrying a copy in the glove compartment of the car is also a wise idea. If you go into the hospital, give copies to the doctors and nurses and other staff who might be involved with decisions concerning critical care. Your goal is to maximize the odds that your Living Will will be considered when actually needed.

In the event that you have a change of heart, it is always possible to cancel a Living Will. An oral revocation is legally sufficient in most states. Still, to avoid any mix-ups, all copies of that Living Will previously given out should be collected and destroyed. A statement explaining that the Living Will is canceled should be written, signed, and dated in the presence of two people. This should eliminate any possible confusion over your true wishes.

The laws governing Living Wills vary from state to state. You'll want to make sure you obtain documents that comply with your particular state's rules. You can obtain state-suitable forms at www.partnershipforcaring.org. You should also speak with an experienced elder-law attorney, and perhaps your physician, to make sure you understand these documents before "signing away your life."

The AARP Legal Counsel for the Elderly has published a forty-page booklet called *Planning for Incapacity: A Self-Help Guide,* for each state and the District of Columbia. The booklets include Living Will and Health Care Durable Power of Attorney forms for your state. To obtain a copy, contact the Legal Counsel for the Elderly, P.O. Box 96474, Washington, DC 10090-6474, and specify your state of residence. There will be a small charge.

Although a trustee under your Revocable Living Trust can provide many valuable services, making important life and death decisions is not one of them. If you don't want "heroic measures" to be taken after you've entered a vegetative state, you'll want and need a Living Will.

Note: If your desire is to be kept alive using all possible measures, you should make a Living Will that says so. This is often called a "Will to Live." Ask your lawyer about this document.

CHAPTER 9

Choosing the
Right Lawyer

An elderly woman went to see her lawyer about a will. After she nervously went through the list of people to whom she wanted to leave her estate, the lawyer said, "Don't worry, just leave it all to me." With a sigh, she responded, "I guess you're right—you'll get it all anyway." For many folks, this lawyer joke has more than a ring of truth to it.

No one wants to spend a fortune on legal fees, and unquestionably Starter Trusts combined with SAFE Trusts are not cheap. But resist the temptation to save money by trying to draft these documents on your own; that would be a very unsafe and unwise idea. SAFE planning is not a do-it-yourself project. If you must dabble, build a bookcase to hold your legal documents. You can live with lopsided bookshelves. But the consequences of an improperly built estate plan can cause your best intentions to topple.

The benefits of a SAFE plan are tremendous, but only if the plan is done right. And without an experienced lawyer, chances are good your plan will not be done correctly or most appropriately to fit your needs.

HOW DO YOU FIND A LAWYER TO PREPARE YOUR SAFE PLAN?

Finding a lawyer is rarely a problem. The challenge is finding the *right* lawyer—ideally an individual who is experienced in the SAFE approach to planning.

Unfortunately, there are a lot of lawyers who handle estate planning as a sideline. They may do divorce, personal injury, or real estate work . . . and they'll do your estate plan too. Estate planning, if done correctly and comprehensively, generally is complicated, and SAFE Trusts are specialized trusts that not just any attorney can throw together. You need a lawyer who specializes in estate planning or elder law, and who has done SAFE Trusts before.

Not all lawyers refer to SAFE Trusts or SAFE planning using these terms, which are trademarked. Other terms sometimes used for these or similar approaches include Family Protection Trusts, Generation Skipping Trusts, and Spendthrift Trusts. The terminology is not as important as the substantive protections and the comprehensive strategy.

To add to the challenge, there are nonlawyers out there trying to do estate planning and trusts for clients. Cookie-cutter trust mills are not for you. Trust me, you might get documents that look, feel, and smell like a trust, but you will *not* get a quality SAFE Trust to fit your needs from a non-lawyer trust production company.

I have seen situations in which people prepared, and paid for, what they thought was a comprehensive plan designed to protect their family, only to find years later—when the protections were actually needed—that the plan did not accomplish the intended results. In fact, in some cases bad documents can make matters worse than if no trust had been created. For just one example, I've seen cases in which parents executed a trust intended to protect an inheritance for a disabled child, only to find that the trust caused the child to lose necessary public benefits like Medicaid.

Where should you begin your search for a lawyer with expertise in SAFE estate planning? Contact a new organization, just being formed, called the Society of American Family Trust and Estate Attorneys

(SAFTEA) at www.SAFTEA.com. Here you will find attorneys who are utilizing comprehensive SAFE planning and creating SAFE Trusts in their law practices. The SAFTEA Web site also contains additional helpful information about SAFE Trusts.

If you still haven't located an attorney in your area, following are ten tips:

Don't:

1. Pick a lawyer at random from the telephone book unless you like playing Russian Roulette.

2. Rely on general advertising. Anyone can advertise, regardless of ability or experience.

Do:

3. Ask your friends; perhaps they've already used a lawyer for SAFE estate planning advice. If they recommend their personal injury lawyer, that lawyer is probably *not* the right attorney to help you with a SAFE Trust, although he or she might be able to recommend someone who can.

4. Ask other professionals whom you trust for any suggestions. Your accountant, doctor, clergyman or clergywoman, or banker might know a lawyer experienced in handling comprehensive SAFE planning. These people often work with estate-planning lawyers and may know a good one.

5. Contact the local chapter of the Alzheimer's Association, the Arthritis Foundation, the Diabetes Association, or one of the other nonprofit "disease" organizations. Personnel in these organizations may know the attorneys who are experienced in SAFE estate planning; some of these organizations even have referral lists. A growing number of hospitals have instituted gerontology units, and doctors or other personnel in these units may be able to recommend a lawyer for SAFE planning work.

6. Ask a professor who teaches probate or estate planning at a law school nearby to recommend lawyers who are "out in the field."

7. Use business contacts. For example, if you or your parent works for a company that hires outside lawyers, ask one of those attorneys for a referral. Because a member of your family works for one of his clients, he is more likely to want to be helpful and assist you with finding a lawyer experienced in doing SAFE planning.

8. Contact local bar associations because they often offer referral services that can provide names of attorneys. These should be used only as a last resort. Lawyers generally get on such lists by paying a small fee—bar associations rarely do any screening at all—so you have no assurance about the competency or expertise of a lawyer.

9. Be cautious about recommendations from anyone who stands to benefit from a referral. For example, a real estate agent, an accountant, or a financial planner may work with one or two lawyers; they refer business to the lawyer and the lawyer refers business to them. Sometimes these referrals are fine, because the referrer wants to make sure you are satisfied; however, your needs may not be the primary concern in such a situation. So don't forgo the screening process discussed below.

10. Check out the National Academy of Elder Law Attorneys. Anyone may join this organization, but it's at least a start. Go to www.naela.org.

HOW DO YOU CHOOSE A LAWYER?

Compile a *list* of names of possible prospects; three to six ought to suffice. Don't just end your search with the first name you're offered.

Now, how do you pick the right lawyer for you from this select group? First, try to narrow the field by learning as much as possible about each attorney's reputation and experience. Ask lawyers you know if they are familiar with the names recommended to you. You can also check the *Martindale-Hubbell Directory*, available in most libraries and online at www.martindale.com.

The *Martindale-Hubbell Directory* online lists most lawyers in the country and gives helpful information about many of them. For example, here's the listing for me (an interpretation will follow):

Armond D. Budish

Member

Budish, Solomon, Steiner & Peck, Ltd.

23240 Chagrin Boulevard, Suite 450

Beachwood, Ohio 44122

(Cuyahoga Co.)

Telephone: 216-765-0123

Facsimile: 216-595-2787

Email: info@budishandsolomon.com

Rated AV

Practice Areas: Elder Law; Litigation; Estate Planning

Admitted: 1977, Maryland; 1979, District of Columbia, Ohio, U.S. District Court for the District of Columbia and U.S. Court of Appeals for the District of Columbia Circuit

Law School: New York University, J.D., cum laude, 1977

College: Swarthmore College, B.A., cum laude, 1974

Member: Cleveland (Chairman, Young Lawyers Section, 1983–1984; Member, Board of Trustees, 1983–1984), Ohio State and American (Member, Executive Council, Young Lawyers Division, 1985–1987) Bar Associations; National Academy of Elder Law Attorneys; Alzheimer's Association (Cleveland Board, Executive Committee, 2003–   )

Biography: Order of the Coif. Root-Tilden Scholar. Associate Editor, New York University Law Review, 1976–1977. Law Clerk to Honorable Aubrey E. Robinson, Jr., Chief Judge, United States District Court for the District of Columbia. Author: "Avoiding the Medicaid Trap," Henry Holt & Co., 1989,

1990, 1995; "Golden Opportunities," Henry Holt & Co., 1992, 1994; "You and the Law," Columns in the Cleveland Plain Dealer, 1982–2006; Columbus Dispatch, 1985–2006. Host, "Golden Opportunities" television show and regular legal commentator, WKYC-TV (NBC). Contributing Editor, Family Circle Magazine, 1988–2006.

Born: Cleveland, Ohio, June 2, 1953

The *Martindale-Hubbell Directory* rates lawyers based on their legal ability and ethical standards, by surveying lawyers and judges in the area where the lawyer practices. These are the only nationally recognized lawyer ratings.

The legal ability ratings are "A" (very high), "B" (high), and "C" (fair). These ratings are based on the lawyer's ability, experience, and nature and length of practice. The ethical rating is a "V" (very high). There is no other ethical rating available; a lawyer receives either a "V" or nothing. So if the lawyer you are considering has an "AV" rating, take that as a major plus. It's important to note that many lawyers, good and bad, are not rated by the *Martindale-Hubbell Directory*. The absence of a rating doesn't necessarily mean that a lawyer is unqualified.

To speed your search, you may go to the Martindale.com home page, and click on the "Location/Area of Practice" area, then go to "Select general areas of practice" and click on "Trust and Estates." Fill in your city, go to your state, then "search." You'll get a pretty complete listing of estate-planning lawyers in your area. Again, this is just a beginning, not an end.

INTERVIEWING AND COMPARISON SHOPPING

Once you have narrowed the field, you should interview the lawyers remaining on your list. Upon arriving at a lawyer's office, you should try not to let the surroundings affect your judgment. A beautiful office might mean that the lawyer got rich from doing great work for clients, but it might also mean that the lawyer's mother is wealthy and decorated the office for him or that the lawyer made a lot of money by overcharging clients.

Nor should you be misled by fancy-looking certificates on the walls. Some of the worst lawyers have the most impressive wall coverings. For example, the lawyer may prominently display a certificate stating that he or she has been admitted to practice before the local federal court or even the United States Supreme Court. Don't be fooled—any lawyer can get one of those with a minimal fee and a few references from lawyers in town. Diplomas may be a little more helpful as they show what schools the lawyer has attended. A certificate from the Order of the Coif means that the lawyer graduated at the top of his or her law school class.

Following is a questionnaire that you can use for guidance when interviewing prospective lawyers. By all means, feel free to modify it to suit your style. *How* the lawyer answers the questions is as important as *what* is said. You should feel comfortable with the lawyer, confident in his or her abilities, and satisfied that he or she understands your needs and will answer your questions clearly and without making you feel that you are wasting his or her time. While we are on the subject of time, it is important that you too be respectful of the attorney's time. By coming prepared with a list of your questions, you can be assured that the meeting will be productive.

SAFE PLANNING LAWYER
INTERVIEW QUESTIONNAIRE

1. HOW MANY PEOPLE HAVE YOU COUNSELED ON ESTATE-PLANNING MATTERS IN THE PAST FIVE YEARS?

_____

_____

2. HOW MANY SAFE TRUSTS HAVE YOU PREPARED IN THE PAST FIVE YEARS? (IF THEY DON'T UNDERSTAND THE TERM SAFE TRUSTS, EXPLAIN WHAT YOU WISH TO ACCOMPLISH; BETTER YET, GIVE THEM A COPY OF THIS BOOK.)

_____

_____

_____

---

3. WILL YOU GIVE ME A LIST OF REFERENCES I MIGHT CONTACT—
CLIENTS FOR WHOM YOU'VE DONE SAFE PLANNING? (THEN CALL
THEM, JUST AS YOU WOULD IF YOU WERE HIRING A PAINTER.)

_____

_____

4. HOW DO YOU STAY UP-TO-DATE ON OUR STATE AND FEDERAL ES-
TATE TAX, MEDICAID, AND CREDITOR-PROTECTION LAWS?

_____

_____

5. WHAT OUTSIDE ACTIVITIES DO YOU PARTICIPATE IN? (IF THE
LAWYER TEACHES ESTATE AND PROBATE LAW AT A LAW SCHOOL,
THAT IS A POSITIVE RECOMMENDATION. THE FACT THAT HE MIGHT BE
ACTIVE IN HIS CHURCH IS NICE, BUT IT'S NOT PERTINENT TO YOU.)

_____

_____

6. WITH WHOM DO YOU CONSULT ON LEGAL QUESTIONS YOU'RE
NOT SURE ABOUT? (A LAWYER SHOULD HAVE OTHER EXPERIENCED
ATTORNEYS, EITHER IN THE OFFICE OR IN THE COMMUNITY, WITH
WHOM HE OR SHE CONSULTS WHEN NECESSARY. NO LAWYER KNOWS
EVERYTHING; IF A LAWYER TELLS YOU OTHERWISE, LOOK ELSE-
WHERE.) _____

_____

7. ARE YOU THE PERSON WHO WILL HANDLE MY MATTER, OR WILL
YOU BE TURNING IT OVER TO SOMEONE ELSE? (YOU MAY ACTUALLY
BE BETTER OFF IF A YOUNGER, LOWER-PRICED ATTORNEY IN THE OF-
FICE HANDLES THE MATTER, AS LONG AS HE OR SHE WILL BE WELL
SUPERVISED.) _____

_____

8. HOW LONG WILL IT TAKE TO PROVIDE ME WITH A SAFE ESTATE
PLAN AND NECESSARY DOCUMENTS? _____

_____

9. WHAT WILL YOUR FEE BE, AND WHAT IS YOUR TIMELINE FOR
PAYMENT? _____

_____

10. WHAT KIND OF FOLLOW-UP DO YOU PROVIDE ONCE A SAFE ES-
TATE PLAN IS DONE? _____

_____

11. HOW DO YOU PREFER I CONTACT YOU—TELEPHONE, E-MAIL?

_____

12. HOW SOON CAN I EXPECT A RESPONSE FROM SOMEONE AFTER
I'VE CONTACTED YOU? _____

_____

13. ARE MY FAMILY MEMBERS WELCOME TO JOIN ME IN OUR
MEETINGS? _____

_____

Questions 1 and 2 are designed to help you gauge the lawyer's experience. You don't want the lawyer to be learning on you. The laws are constantly changing, so review the lawyer's answer to question 4 to make sure
he or she is taking reasonable steps to keep up-to-date.

Questions 8 and 9 will tell you how long the lawyer will take to prepare
your plan, and what it will cost. Get firm answers; make sure there are no
unpleasant surprises later. A SAFE plan typically will not be a one-time,
static program, but instead may require regular follow-ups.

Question 10 will indicate how the lawyer plans to keep your planning current. One of the chief aggravations clients express is the lack of prompt responses when they call. Talk about the lawyer's practices in advance of retaining him or her.

The answers that the lawyer provides to these questions should help you pick a lawyer who is capable, experienced, and comfortable for you to work with.

PART IV

Other Issues
to Consider

CHAPTER 10

What Are
the Downsides?

A s we all know, in real life nothing is perfect, and that includes SAFE Trusts. By now you have seen the tremendous
benefits and protections that SAFE Trusts offer. They are
not for everyone, however, and it's important to understand the
downsides too. But before we begin, let's start on a positive
note and quickly review the benefits.

Probably the biggest misconception about trusts concerns
control over your assets while you're alive. Don't get confused.
When you set up a SAFE Trust, it is almost always joined with
a Starter Trust. And with most of the Starter Trusts, *you* can be
the trustee and maintain control of your assets throughout your
lifetime. Lots of folks have the mistaken notion that they lose
control over trust assets, that a bank takes over. That's just not
true. Banks can serve as trustees, and in some cases that's appropriate (see Chapter 7). But in the vast majority of cases
people choose to be their own trustees. And in that case, you

keep control. So loss of control during your lifetime is not a valid reason to forgo a Starter Trust/SAFE Trust arrangement.

Starter Trust/SAFE Trust combinations provide an efficient and private means for leaving assets at death, avoiding probate, cutting or eliminating death taxes, and keeping the inheritance away from your children's spouses and creditors. So no negatives there.

And your children can serve as their own trustees of the SAFE Trusts. So they can maintain control and take money as they need it, without having to ask anyone else's permission. No problem there either.

So what are the negatives? There are four.

Negative 1: Complexity

You've probably already figured this one out. Setting up Starter Trusts that distribute to SAFE Trusts, which continue for the lifetimes of the children, is definitely not as simple as just leaving the assets outright to the children at your death.

This added complexity won't affect *you*—don't worry about that. As mentioned above, most SAFE Trusts follow simple Revocable Living Trusts. The SAFE Trusts don't come into play until you die.

After you're gone, your children's inheritances will distribute to SAFE Trusts. Even though your children can be in control, it's still not quite as easy as having the money dropped directly into their pockets. As discussed, each SAFE Trust will require a separate tax ID number (like a Social Security number for the trust) and a separate income tax return each year. But the tax return usually is pretty simple, particularly if the income is paid out to the children.

Although your children can control their SAFE Trusts, you must include provisions for alternate/successor trustees to take over if your child becomes incapacitated or deceased. And you must include provisions for paying out the remaining assets when your children die. All these provisions in your SAFE plan create more complexity than simply leaving an inheritance directly to your kids.

Administering a SAFE Trust also is more involved than managing the funds in your own name. Assets in the SAFE Trust receive many protections, but once they are distributed from the trust to your children or others, the protections are gone. So let's say a creditor has obtained a judgment against your son. While the creditor can't reach into the SAFE Trust, the creditor *can* grab assets distributed from the SAFE Trust to your son's personal bank account. So to maximize the benefits of the trust, your son's bills, to the extent possible, would be paid directly from the SAFE Trust, with the money never going into his accounts. While that's more complicated, it's also more protective.

Negative 2: Limit on Children's Access

I've explained that, after you're gone, your Revocable Living Trust will pass the assets into a SAFE Trust for each of your children. At that point, your children can be in charge, they can handle the investments, and they can take money as they need it. They have broad access and control. But there are usually limits.

Typically your children can freely take all the income generated by the investments. But to get all the benefits for your children that the SAFE Trust has to offer, you'll have to limit the children's access to the principal to their "reasonable needs," as appropriate for their standard of living. To maximize the SAFE protections, they cannot take principal for things that are not "needs."

How are "needs" defined? The law generally says "needs" include food, clothing, shelter (rent or mortgage payments, or principal to buy a home), transportation, health care, entertainment, travel, and education. This can be very broad, but it's not unlimited. For example, if your child goes to Florida for a week each year, that can probably be paid from the SAFE Trust. But a trip around the world that costs ten times more than their prior vacations typically cannot come from the trust monies. If your child buys a new Chevy every four years, the next Camaro can be paid from the trust. But a new Rolls-Royce is probably too much.

If this bothers you, then you can give your children unlimited access to the principal. And the children still get *most* of the benefits of the SAFE Trust. For example, it will still avoid probate, and in most states it will still protect against the child's spouse grabbing the assets when the child dies. But your children may lose the divorce and creditor protections. That's because a court may say that if your child has complete access and control, the trust assets are his, just the same as they would have been without the SAFE Trust, and for that reason they should be shared with a spouse or creditor. Also note that for a SAFE Trust to insulate your child's inheritance from lawsuits and creditors, in some states your child will have to step down as trustee and relinquish control.

Negative 3: Income Tax

While you serve as trustee of your Revocable Living Trust, there is absolutely no income tax concern. The trust uses your Social Security number, and any income (e.g., interest, dividends, rents) generated by investments in the trust is reported as your income, just exactly as it was before the trust was established. There's no separate or different income tax return—just use your own personal return.

Even if you become incapacitated and another person steps in as alternate trustee, there's no income tax problem. The income is still reported on your personal income tax return.

When you die, and your assets pass into the SAFE Trusts for the children, each SAFE Trust will get its own tax identification number from the IRS. Each SAFE Trust will have to have its own annual income tax return.

If the interest or dividends are paid out to the beneficiary (your children or grandchildren), the SAFE Trust will pay no income tax. The income would just be shown as a "pass-through" to the kid, or grandkid, on the SAFE Trust tax return. In that case, it would be the children or grandchildren who would then put the income on their personal income tax returns and pay tax at their personal rates, just as they would if the assets which generate the income were in their own personal names. So far, there's still no negative.

The only negative comes if the assets in the children's SAFE Trusts generate income that is *retained* in the SAFE Trusts and not paid out to the children or grandchildren. In that case, and only in that case, would the SAFE Trust show the income on its own tax return and pay its own income tax. That's where the negative comes in, because the income tax rates that apply to SAFE Trusts are generally somewhat higher than people's personal income tax rates. The difference might be as much as about 20 percent.

The most common ways around this extra income tax are to pay out the income from the trust or to invest trust assets in tax-deferred, tax-free, or capital-growth vehicles. For example, if your child (as trustee of his SAFE Trust) decides to invest in growth stocks or mutual funds generating little or no income, the income tax problem goes away; when the appreciated investments are sold, the trust will pay capital gains tax at the same rates that individuals pay (with no penalty even though they are in the trust). If your child invests in tax-free bonds, again the income tax penalty can be eliminated.

Negative 4: Cost

This is the biggest downside to a SAFE Trust. The costs will vary across the country. Just as a mansion in Shaker Heights, Ohio, might be a third of the price of a comparable home in Boston or in Southern California, the same holds true for the cost of legal documents in various locales. Having said that, I will provide a ballpark estimate: a basic Starter Trust combined with a SAFE Trust will probably run anywhere from $3,000 to $6,000. And the cost can go much higher if multiple trusts are combined. I've seen SAFE Trust combinations cost as much as $20,000, but that's rare.

Can you get around these costs by doing the documents yourself? I've already said it before, and I'll say it again: *No!* This is not a do-it-yourself area. If a SAFE Trust is not done correctly, you can create problems for your family for years to come, without getting the desired benefits.

At these prices, the obvious question then becomes: Is it worth the cost? For some folks the answer is no, and for many the answer is yes. Here are some guidelines to consider as you weigh the pros and cons.

Go back to the SAFE Assessment Tool that you filled out in Chapter 2. Think about the concerns and goals identified by your answers to the questions, and the issues we discussed in the following chapters.

Would you like to avoid probate? A Revocable Living Trust/SAFE Trust combination accomplishes that goal. But there are other much less expensive techniques to avoid probate. As discussed in Chapter 3, you can name joint owners or beneficiaries on your assets, for little or no cost. And that avoids probate.

If probate avoidance is your *sole* concern, then a Revocable Living Trust/SAFE Trust combination may not be worth the cost. But a SAFE

Trust offers many more benefits. For example, if your answers to the SAT pointed up concerns you have about a child's spouse, and you don't want your child's inheritance to end up with the child's spouse, then you absolutely should do a SAFE Trust. In one case that I handled, the nicest woman in the world asked me for help. She didn't have a large estate, but she had worked hard for what she had. She loved her daughter dearly. She absolutely hated her daughter's husband, however. He didn't treat his wife (my client's daughter) nicely, and was outright nasty to my client. She was willing to spend $3,000 for a Revocable Living Trust/SAFE Trust to make sure her daughter's husband would never see a penny of the inheritance.

If your answers to the SAT indicate you are concerned about a disabled child, a Special Needs SAFE Trust is very important. If you're in a second marriage and you want to allow your spouse to remain living in the home when you die, yet you also want the home to go to *your* children, not to your spouse's kids, upon his death, then you should have a Marital Trust/ SAFE Trust. If you and your spouse have a very large estate, an A-B Trust/SAFE Trust combination can save you hundreds of thousands of dollars in federal death taxes. In all of these cases, and in many more, an investment of several thousand dollars is well worth the cost.

The key is to find a trustworthy estate planning attorney who will review your answers to the SAT, will help you sort out your priorities, and will talk with you about both the benefits *and* the negatives of a SAFE Trust for your unique circumstances. And make no mistake: each person's situation *is* unique. SAFE Trusts are really terrific planning tools, but they're not perfect for everyone. Nothing ever is.

CHAPTER 11

What Happens
at Death?

Y ou and your spouse have shown good foresight and set up a SAFE plan, which includes a Revocable Living Trust, to pour into a SAFE Trust. The sad reality is that a death will trigger the implementation of your plans. When a spouse dies, what should you do? No one likes to consider this. Nevertheless, it is essential to review the numerous unpleasant but important tasks that must still be undertaken, even with the best advance planning.

When your spouse's assets are in a trust, the process at his death will be much simpler, easier, and less expensive than if the assets were in his individual name. But the surviving spouse must still take some required actions. Here's a to-do checklist.

1. ***Find all burial and funeral papers.*** Check to see if the funeral has been prearranged and prepaid. Once is enough: you don't need to plan and pay twice.

2. *Contact Social Security and the pension administrator.* Immediately contact Social Security and the administrator of your spouse's pension plan to let them know he's died. This has nothing to do with the trust, but it's important. If Social Security and the pension administrator are not informed, they may continue to send your spouse's checks, and you may spend the money (that's not rightfully yours). Eventually, you'll face a hardship when they demand that you return the overpayments.

3. *Make a list of all the assets.* You'll need to know exactly what's in your spouse's name, your spouse's Starter Trust, your name, and your trust (if you have a separate trust). For assets in your spouse's name, but not in a trust, you'll also need to check on the beneficiary designations. Any assets you discover in your spouse's name alone, not in a trust, with no joint owner and no beneficiary, are likely to require probate— unfortunately.

4. *Contact your family's professionals.* Speak with your family attorney, accountant, and financial adviser, and ask for help.

5. *Do not make any immediate, drastic financial changes.* You'll need to get control of your finances. After you've determined all of your assets, you'll need to make a budget, and compare your anticipated income with your expected expenses. If your income is not going to be sufficient to cover your costs, then you may have to change your investments to generate more income, or possibly find employment. And you'll have to determine whether it's feasible to cut expenses.

   By all means, face the challenges. But avoid making any drastic decisions too hastily. Don't be surprised if you suddenly start receiving "friendly" solicitations from all sorts of financial salesmen offering to help and pushing to sell you new investments. These may or may not be appropriate. You should take things slowly. Learn about your existing investments, research your alternatives, get names of trustworthy financial professionals from friends, and talk with several of them. Don't let anyone push you into making significant investment changes too quickly.

6. ***Get a tax ID number for your spouse's trust.*** If your spouse had his own trust, perhaps an A-B Trust or a Marital Trust, coupled with a SAFE Trust, at his death you'll probably need to get a tax ID number for his trust. The tax ID number takes the place of his Social Security number (which ends when he or she dies). Get the tax ID number from the IRS (or ask your lawyer or accountant to get it). You'll have to give the new tax ID number to all the banks and brokers holding his trust assets, and probably a death certificate as well showing that your spouse has died. You can get death certificates from the local coroner's office, or perhaps from the funeral home.

7. ***Allocate your spouse's assets as the trust requires.*** If your spouse created an A-B or a Marital Starter Trust, the assets in his trust will have to be allocated in accordance with the terms of that trust.

    Let's say your spouse created an A-B Starter Trust, and provided that up to $2 million would go into the B trust at his death (for tax savings), the rest into the A trust. At his death, the establishment of two separate trusts will be triggered, an A and a B, and up to $2 million would have to be put into the name of the trustee of his B trust. The rest would go into the name of the trustee of his A trust. Most likely, you'll be the trustee of both his A and B trusts.

    And if certain assets were to pass directly to the children, other family members, or charities, then those distributions would also have to be satisfied. The trustee (usually the surviving spouse) must follow the terms of the trust and send the assets to the right people and places.

8. ***Prepare a federal estate tax return if necessary.*** Total all the assets in your spouse's name and trust. If he's on any accounts or real estate jointly with you, include half the amount. Also include the death benefits of any life insurance that he owned.

    If the total exceeds the current death tax exemption, right now $2 million, then you'll have to do a federal estate tax return. Don't panic, though—if the assets are in a properly set-up A-B Trust, or if you're the beneficiary, there won't be any tax to pay. But you still must complete and file the return. Usually a lawyer or accountant should do these for you.

9. ***Prepare a state estate tax return if needed.*** You'll have to check to see whether your state has its own death tax. If so, and your spouse was over that limit, then you'll need to do a state estate tax return.

10. ***Check your spouse's beneficiary designations.*** In most cases, your spouse's IRAs, 401(k)s, annuities, pension, and profit-sharing plans will name you as primary beneficiary. You should contact the plan administrator and your attorney to decide how to handle the account(s). Most people roll the accounts directly into their own IRAs.

    Don't forget to add a new beneficiary at that time. In most cases, you'll want to have your Retirement Fund SAFE Trust as beneficiary (see Chapter 4). And you can name the same trust as beneficiary of your own retirement accounts, in place of your late spouse.

11. ***Change your trustee and agents.*** You've probably named your spouse as the person to handle your affairs as alternate trustee of your trust, executor of your Pourover Will, and agent under your Financial and Health Care Durable Powers of Attorney. If your spouse is no longer alive, your next-in-line alternate won't be able to step in without first showing a death certificate for your late spouse. That can be a hassle and cause unnecessary delays. If you get a divorce, but fail to remove your ex-spouse as alternate trustee or agent, that could be a disaster. (Some states automatically remove an ex-spouse, but others don't.) *Soon* after your spouse dies (or after there's a divorce), call your lawyer to set a meeting to update your trust and related documents to remove your spouse.

12. ***Check health care coverage.*** Perhaps the biggest unexpected strain on your budget after the death of a spouse (or a divorce) will be the costs of health care. If you've been covered under a spouse's policy, you now may have to get your own. Do this quickly. You can't afford to go uncovered, and if you become ill in the interim, you may never get

coverage. If you find yourself having trouble qualifying for coverage, contact a professional insurance agent specializing in health coverage, and possibly a lawyer specializing in COBRA (which protects your right to purchase insurance temporarily after your employment terminates), Medicare, and Medicaid as well.

The most important advice to follow after becoming suddenly single is: Don't panic. You don't have to face all these legal and financial decisions alone. Find an *experienced* and *trustworthy* lawyer and financial consultant to help guide you through this new, uncertain period. Better yet, don't wait until tragedy strikes. Take the time *now* to think about whom you'd like to work with on these matters. With their advice, and the support of friends and family, you will be able to create a well-thought-out plan of action that won't cause you further pain down the road.

Conclusion

I f the late Beatle John Lennon had prepared a SAFE Trust, Yoko might not be riding in a limo while John's son Julian complains about his meager inheritance.

If former U.S. Supreme Court Justice Warren Burger had created a SAFE Trust, his children might have avoided thousands of dollars in costs and taxes at his death.

If Lucky Strike cigarette magnate James "Buck" Duke had signed a SAFE Trust, his daughter's butler might not have struck it lucky by gaining much of the estate.

If George Huntington Hartford, founder of the Great Atlantic & Pacific Tea Company (A&P), had made a SAFE Trust, his grandson might not have been able to squander most of his inheritance by stocking his shelves with women, drugs, and bad investments.

If Joe Robbie had done a SAFE Trust, his family might still be sitting on the fifty-yard line watching their dad's football team, the Miami Dolphins, play in their dad's stadium.

And if J. Howard Marshall had made a SAFE Trust, his son Pierce might have been able to relax watching his late father's wife make a fool of herself on television, instead of battling Anna Nicole Smith in court.

Even the rich and famous, people who can afford the best lawyers in the country, make costly, sometimes tragic mistakes with their estate planning. For the nonrich and nonfamous, it's easy to create a big mess for your family—unintentionally.

Do you want your child's spouse or creditors to wind up with *your* hard-earned savings and home? Are you convinced that your children and grandchildren will manage their inheritance wisely? Would you like to make Uncle Sam a major beneficiary of your estate? If the answer to any of these questions is no, you must consider a SAFE plan.

SAFE planning provides comprehensive, practical solutions to the most common problems lurking for you and your family. A will, and even a standard Revocable Living Trust, is no longer enough. These twentieth-century documents are often not sufficient to keep your family safe and financially secure in the twenty-first century.

It's time to put a plan in place that can establish the safeguards for your family against a miserable in-law, a spendthrift heir, an aggressive creditor, and a grabby tax collector. It's time to demonstrate the same commitment that enabled you to raise your family, create a nest egg, and build your retirement. It's time—right now—for a SAFE plan!

Index

About the Author

Armond D. Budish

For more than twenty years, Armond D. Budish has been assisting families in protecting their homes and life savings, and in fulfilling their dreams, through estate planning. He has been a pioneer in the field of elder law, and has developed the SAFE approach to estate planning.

After graduating from Swarthmore College (with honors) and New York University Law School (*Law Review*, Order of the Coif), and clerking for the Honorable Aubrey E. Robinson Jr. in Washington, D.C., Armond returned home to Cleveland, Ohio, to practice law. For twenty-four years, he wrote a consumer-law newspaper column (*The Cleveland Plain Dealer* and *Columbus Dispatch*), and he became a contributing editor to *Family Circle* magazine; in these publications he provided helpful tips and advice.

Armond D. Budish "wrote the book" on elder law. In 1989, *Avoiding the Medicaid Trap: How to Beat the Catastrophic Costs of Nursing Home Care* (Henry Holt, 1989, 1990, 1995) was first published, followed in 1992 by *Golden Opportunities: Hundreds of Money-Making, Money-Saving Gems for Anyone over Fifty* (Henry Holt, 1992, 1994). These books became the national bibles on family asset maximization and protection. For the last eight years, Armond has produced and hosted the television show *Golden Opportunities*, a consumer-oriented, information-packed program airing on Sunday mornings on Cleveland's NBC affiliate, TV-3.

Armond D. Budish is a founding partner in the law firm of Budish, Solomon, Steiner & Peck. He and his partners have helped thousands of people plan for their futures and reach their goals for themselves and their families.

Armond D. Budish has always been committed to public service. In furtherance of that goal, he has just been elected to the Ohio House of Representatives.

Amy J. Budish

While not listed as a coauthor, Armond's wife, Amy, has been his partner in the writing, editing, and development of this book. Amy previously cowrote *Avoiding the Medicaid Trap* and *Golden Opportunities* with her husband. She has a master's degree in consumer education. Her employment has included stints as consumer affairs specialist in the White House for President Jimmy Carter's special assistant for consumer affairs, Esther Peterson, as well as in Ohio Attorney General Lee Fisher's office. She also served as consumer affairs liaison for U.S. Senator Howard Metzenbaum. Amy has edited Armond's consumer-law newspaper columns and magazine articles for twenty-four years, as well as written for *Family Circle* magazine, and produces and writes the television program *Golden Opportunities*. The reason you can read *Why Wills Won't Work* so easily? Amy Budish translates Armond's legalese into plain English that everyone can understand.